# Around The Bend –
# One L of a Job

## Vincent Ryan

For
Dors and Joe

Thank you Reina for your love, support and
encouragement throughout

www.thevincentryan.com

Facebook:       TheVincent Ryan

Twitter:        @TheVincentRyan

## About the Author

In addition to his continued career as a Driving Instructor, Vincent Ryan has a long established love of language and languages speaking German, Dutch and Spanish to varying degrees and teaching English as a foreign language.

Originally from west London, he now lives with his wife in a small village in Dorset and enjoys music, reading and travel.

# Chapter 1 – Changing Direction

I jumped excitedly onto the pavement and the bus drew away from my vision to reveal the proud sign above the otherwise anonymous office door announce, The Driving Instructor Centre Kingston South... The D.I.C.K.S!

My heart sank and all my schoolboy insecurities flooded back as I imagined the reaction of my friends when I told them where I was studying. Nonetheless I had an appointment and I was going to keep it.

Having spoken my name clearly and politely into the small aluminium entry phone grill I received no reply other than an elongated buzz inviting me in. Pushing the resistance-free door my heart began to race again and I realised that I was nervous! What an idiot I told myself. It's not a job interview it's a sales pitch from THEM to get me to BUY their course. And I'm nervous!

Once inside, my self-ridicule subsided and I squeezed into the jerky and claustrophobic lift. Other than the two grey, narrow doors, each wall was completely mirrored to give the impression of much needed space and, presumably, to reduce the risk of panic attacks. However, looking up (as one always does in a lift, even when you are in there) I glimpsed my thinning pate in the, slightly unnerving, ceiling mirror and quickly looked back to my freshly shined shoes. Some things are too painful to confront. I urgently needed to find something else to occupy my mind for the estimated 30 second journey to floor four and so began reading anything and everything displayed in the cabin.

"Lift Receiver in Emergency" one lonely red-lettered plastic plaque announced earnestly above an empty recess from which a short, snipped black cable hung.

Another ordered: "Do Not Jump" like the irrational swimming pool rule and a third simply stated, "Maximum Load 120kg" – about one and a half people I calculated!

A final jolt, accompanied by a ping announced the opening doors.

Three, cheaply suited men smiling in exactly the way they had been told to, greeted me with the sincerity of estate agents. These must be The D.I.C.K.S., I thought to myself and my smile matched theirs.

Whilst rooted to the spot in the narrowest part of the doorway, all three thrust their right arms forward, like searching tentacles, to shake my hand then drew me, as if through a crowded train carriage, past them and into the frosted glass and whiteboard office behind them.

Their spoken welcomes blurred together – to which, somewhat confused, I just nodded and smiled – but halted abruptly once I was in the office. Their well-rehearsed, action-packed, "greet" contrasted greatly with the four glum faces seated in the reception room.

Buoyed by the earlier welcome committee I had considered continuing the "handshake and smile" routine but, upon glimpsing my fellow pupils' slumped seated body language and averted eyes (each one was staring at a different, light-blue, coffee-stained nylon floor tile!), I decided to scrap the idea.

Of the four, one immediately stood out. He was about twice the breadth of the rest of us, half the height, and cropped, patchy hair like stumps in a cornfield just after harvesting. Not that any of us would have told him so, such was his aura! The twisting and writhing blue and black tattoos up his jaw line and from his short sleeves to his wrists also sent a signal and I began to understand why the other, less threatening, three were avoiding any eye contact at all.

I agreed with their decision and sat beside him to be sure of not looking wrongly at him and sparking an ugly incident.

There was silence in the room and the only movement came from the occasional rubbing of the fat man's nail-bitten fingers over his head and face to hide his yawning.

The other three were grey-faced individuals, apparently in need of some of my neighbour's calories and all dressed for obscurity.

Between them they wore once-white T-shirts, a well-worn and bobbly dark blue hoody with chewed drawstrings, an array of probably fake Reebok, Adidas and Hilfiger tracksuit bottoms and all with trainers which seemed to be the only item, including themselves, of which any care had been taken.

I suddenly panicked! Was I in a job centre?

My brief fears were allayed by,

"'Ello Babes!" as Debbie, The D.I.C.K.S. receptionist, with her Barbara Windsor voice, bounced into the room.

A big girl, Debbie seemed to enjoy displaying the fact and relished the attention five pairs of eyes immediately afforded her.

Suddenly the three prospective driving instructors opposite me began to shift nervously in their low, square, blue-cushioned seats. Their eyes darting insecurely between Debbie's well-displayed chest and my tattooed neighbour for his reaction. He too was suddenly awakened from his repeated yawning and beamed a gold-filled toothy grin from his ever-reddening face by Debbie's sudden appearance.

But just as the atmosphere began to rise with Debbie's warm front, in swept the drizzle that was to be our trainer. Ethan or, as he introduced himself in his best elongated, pseudo-posh "Boycie" voice, "Ee-fun", welcomed us again, transparently reciting the scripted text for day one pupils, enhancing the training before us with the excitement of a children's magic entertainer that was probably genuine when he first delivered it several hundred times ago. He explained that he was to be our trainer for today and that he hoped that we would enjoy ourselves.

Once again I looked around the room and had my doubts.

The day continued in this, local radio "yes indeedee", vein and from which we learned that we were to be tested on our theory questions and hazard perception videos (this was known as Part 1), would have to re-take a driving test, Part 2, and go through a role-play test for instructional techniques before we reached the goal of ADI (Approved Driving Instructor). This was the dreaded Part 3.

At this news a collective draw of breath whistled through the room and our faces betrayed our reservations. This hadn't been mentioned before we had signed, and more importantly paid, up!

## Part 1

Ethan, not being able to be as daft as he looked or sounded, picked up on the mood and reassured us that it would not be a problem for experienced drivers like us and even threw in a couple of theory test questions as examples.

"Listen," he smiled and flicked apparently randomly through the Theory Test book and read the first question:

"Tailgating means…

1   Using the rear door of a hatchback car.
2   Reversing into a parking space *(he snorted and shook his head in mock disbelief)*
3   Following another vehicle too closely *(he slowed the pace of his reading and look directly at us all in emphasis)*
4   Driving with the rear fog lights on.

"not much too difficult there," he laughed, snapping the thick paperback closed but, from the weak reaction from his audience, he felt the need to add "I hope."

Nevertheless a distant alarm bell began to ring with me although I allowed myself to continue to be swept along with Ethan's almost real enthusiasm.

"How easy is that then?" he joked, but one or two of my classmates didn't seem to find it easy at all and became noticeably paler.

Moving swiftly on, Ethan distracted us with our course books. Five, thick A4 sized books, all proudly bearing the Driving Instructor Centre Kingston South name and logo, were presented to us.

Was I the only one to inwardly giggle at the abbreviation?

None of the other four sniggered or even raised an eyebrow.

Ethan even frequently referred to the company by spelling out a shortened version of the title, "The Dee Eye See" but still no reaction from anyone else. Was he taking the mickey? Was this a set-up or a test and he was waiting for someone to mention it? If he was, I was too much of a coward to allow it to be me and the others looked either too dim or were clearly more mature than me, so he was to be disappointed.

"All you need to know is in these…" Ethan tapped a pile of folder-books and our collective silence begged one same question – If it was all so bloody simple, why did it need five books to cover it?

"Off ya go now and study 'em at home," he chirped, too obviously happy to hasten us out of the classroom. "When ya feel confident enough to do ya test, give us a call and we'll book ya in for a mock test."

Top training, I thought, but obediently shuffled out behind the other four back into the reception area and past Debbie who, in the meantime had apparently felt the cold and had pulled on a roll-neck sweater. It made me quietly laugh at the other four as they, nevertheless, still couldn't resist a glance at her now, hidden, chest until I, despondently, caught myself victim of the same reflex.

Once back out into the hallway we were again faced by the doors of the one-and-a-half-man lift. Maybe two of the other three might squeeze in together but if the tattooed, neck-less man got there first, and I suspected he would, then there was no chance for anyone else so I decided to walk the eight, short flights down.

I half pushed, half leant through the scuffed grey swing doors to the staircase and allowed my legs to loosely tap-tap their way down the stone steps, echoing around the painted brick walls. When I reached the comparative luxury of the green, wiry carpet of the ground floor entry hall I passed the sealed lift doors and glanced up at the illuminated floor numbers above them. Both 2 and 3 were lit and a faint tapping could be heard from the shaft above.

Despite my cynicism, the theory test did indeed prove to be as simple as Ethan had described. I didn't quite get the "tailgating" question he had highlighted but I *was* asked,

"What style of driving causes increased risk to everyone?"

A    Considerate.
B    Defensive.
C    Competitive.
D    Responsible.

Now, even if you are the most racey of boy racers, if you came up with any other answer than C, I suggest you give up driving immediately until you come to your senses. Do it for the sake of your, and more importantly my, continued health.

The test centre was an old office in the 3rd floor of an anonymous concrete tower block in the centre of Kingston.

Once cleared and searched by the airport-style security guard, I then had to deposit all my possessions into a designated locker and, oddly enough and in line with the airport theme, I succumbed to the impulse to remove my shoes and put them in the locker too. Only when I had handed over the key to the warden-like woman behind the well-worn desk did I realise I was missing my shoes, but by then it was too late.

I was escorted to my prison-visit-style booth where an ancient PC, with a screen the size of a large stamp, stood ready to put me through my paces. I slipped on the, disconcertingly, warm and slightly damp, Radio 1 DJ, 1968 model headphones, partly to block out the background noise, but mainly to allow me to hear the questions, just in case I couldn't read!

The thought then flashed through my otherwise vacant mind that if they had thought of this eventuality and hadn't wanted to discriminate against any non-readers, then how had they expected that same person to have learned all the 900 plus questions and answers in the first place? Can you imagine how dull a CD with these questions and answers would be to work with for practice? Just what every illiterate 17 year old wants to find in his/her pile of birthday presents.

The moment I clicked on my first question, the on-screen clock started counting down my one hour and suddenly I felt nervous. Felt the pressure against the clock.

Twenty-two minutes later I had completed all the questions, checked them all a second time and then had plenty of time for doubt to set in. Had I misunderstood something?

I peered sneakily over the pegboard partition to my cubicle at my other, still beavering, co-test takers but none of them seemed to have already finished and then I noticed the extra from "Prisoner Cell Block H" glaring over her heavy, square-rimmed glasses at me.

I slunk instinctively like a naughty schoolboy, back below the level of the booth wall but clearly heard (and felt) the boom of her voice roar, "I shall take that as a sign that you have finished" both through my bean-can headphones and through the flimsy divide of the booth frame. With that, a flash extinguished my humming screen to a small white dot in its centre.

"I wouldn't like to think you were cheating," she accused.

I thought about defending myself, pleading my innocence, but saw the futility and, not wanting to dig any bigger hole than I already seemed to be teetering on the edge of, I stayed silent.

Looking guilty, being a price worth paying if I could get out of here quickly and without further embarrassment, I made my awkward way silently back to the "matron's" front desk and retrieved the key to my locker. She distastefully frowned down at my sock-clad feet as she dropped the key into my palm.

I collected my few belongings – mobile phone, credit card wallet, two fivers and some loose change... and my shoes – and felt even more like I was being released after a night in the cells.

The square, irritated invigilator then silently waved two sheets of A4 paper at me as I left the office. One word leapt from the page at me – "Passed".

## Part 2

"Morning! I'm Quentin Prout." The tall, rake-like figure craned over me as I sat. "I'm going to be your instructor for today's Part 2, day one," he announced in a clipped fashion that immediately presented contradictions to the listener.

Why did he pronounce that word oddly? Does he have an accent? Is he really well spoken or is he aspiring to cover a colloquial accent with a more appropriate one for a – as the black embossed letters on his white plastic, rectangular badge proudly proclaimed – Senior Instructor Master?

Whatever the reason, from his first sentence his diction irritated. Specifically his Ts and Ss. The T in *Quentin* was fired, by his tongue, from between his two front teeth, following a brief pause after the Quen. Apparently to gather momentum.

This was also the case for *question* which became "ques-tee-on" and *issue* slid lispingly and snake like into "ith-see-oo".

My preoccupation with Quentin filled our short walk to the car and I found myself behind the wheel of a new, but rather shabby, Vauxhall Astra whilst my instructor carefully and precisely placed the large plastic L plate pyramid on the roof. Now I felt nervous.

After more than 30 years of trouble-free and clean licence driving, I felt like a shaky 17 year old on his first lesson.

Once secured behind his seat belt, Quentin spoke again. "Today we will begin our Part 2, Driving Ability course," he slowly delivered another well-practised script. His meticulous monologue (including many Ts and Ss!) irked for several long minutes but, when I made the mistake of attempting to join what I assumed until that point was a conversation, Quentin stopped mid-sentence, raised his right palm between our faces and closed his eyes until my words were halted.

This was going to be a long few hours!

And so it proved.

At the end of our three – yes THREE! – hour lesson I knew just two things. One, for all my 30-plus years experience, I knew nothing and two, Quentin had really enjoyed telling me so.

Before we had even left the extremely tight, walled car park, indeed before I had driven out of the parking space, Quentin had "dualled" me. From the very first minute he had managed to emasculate me as a driver by immediately taking the control away with the dual controls and bringing us to an abrupt stop.

I felt strangely embarrassed, humiliated like a naughty schoolboy asked to stand up and read out loud his homework when the teacher knew all along that he hadn't done it.

"Your observations before moving were far from adequate," he smarmed with an attitude which betrayed the fact that he set that trap for me.

Back in the same parking space at the end of the lesson Quentin delighted in delivering his round-up of, what I considered had been, a driving disaster. It included condescending tones and such sarcasm as:

"Well, not too bad for someone who learned *so* long ago."

"You failed to look sufficiently when approaching junctions. Are you sure you've never had an accident?" and,

"Who taught you then? Someone with a stiff neck? You never move your head when looking in the mirrors."

Thoroughly beaten and resentful of my companion for the morning, I took some comfort in the fact that the whole demeaning experience was over... for the time being.

We arrived silently back in the office waiting room and I saw the similarly shattered faces of my co-pupils.

Quentin laughed, just for a second dropping his aloof guard.

"Never mind. We'll knock you into shape over the next twenty weeks or so!"

Our expressions dropped further than we believed possible.

"Twenty weeks?" I gasped.

"Yep," Quentin chirped, "You're one of my projects until the summer. See you next week," and disappeared into the nearest office.

Dejected by my failings as a driver and angered at what I was beginning to fear was a bit of a scam, I brooded on the bus ride home as to the wisdom of my choice of career change.

I even tried to hide my disappointment in myself from my wife by assuring her, in my best fake up-beat voice, that the drive was "okay" and, although admitting that Quentin was a bit odd, I was looking forward to getting through the training.

I doubt if my acting convinced her but, as usual, she diplomatically remained silent. Nevertheless I plodded on and religiously bit the bullet each week to get my Part 2 done.

As the weeks went on however, I found it increasingly difficult to get my preferred morning lessons with Quentin. Each time I called to book I was told by Debbie, whose telephone manner was equally as bouncy, that Quentin only had afternoon sessions available.

Not a major problem I thought, I could be flexible for a couple of weeks and so fixed a few PM sessions until I could re-adjust to the more convenient mornings. In fact I talked myself into believing that the early afternoon might be a good time for driving.

"Hello Vincent," announced behind me, in familiar tones, Quentin's arrival in the waiting room and was strangely accompanied by a rogue smirk from one of the other waiting pupils who tried to pass it off as a sneeze when Quentin flashed a black cloud thunderbolt of a glare at him.

Our walk to the tatty, dark blue Astra was regularly silent and we followed the routine of taking to the driver's seat whilst Quentin gently placed the "L Box" on the car roof before taking the front seat beside me.

"Hopefully you have had the chance to practise? That should help you adhere to the rules of the Highway Code this time."

For once the attempt at his routine crushing sarcasm, at the beginning of the lesson, was in vain however. The huffing aitches of which there were suspiciously very many, held the power at that moment.

An unmistakeable blast of fish slapped my face, deafening my ears to his words, stinging my eyes and stripping the lining from my nostrils. The gagging reflex frequently interrupted the remainder of that lesson as I concentrated on holding my breath as long as possible and never facing my passenger. These two measures reduced the impact of his cat-like exhalations but failed to help me escape the heavy, hanging and faintly metallic hum which completely filled the cabin and convinced me that he had eaten at least one whole fish! Raw!

The earlier smirk from my fellow student was evidently explained, as was his constant availability only in the afternoons. Quentin Prout was quietly known as Quentin Trout for his weakness for fish sandwich lunches.

The weeks and modules slowly crept past and I became aware of and wise to Quentin and his quirks. After several months I began to feel confident enough to handle his attempts to engineer awkward driving situations for me and in my ability to negotiate them successfully.

I even started to, dare I say it, look forward to and enjoy my weekly lessons until one unremarkable spring morning in the D.I.C.K.S. reception office (even now it still makes the schoolboy in me snigger!) when I was addressed by an unfamiliar and uninspiring voice.

"We're having to double up today," he sighed.

I glanced, open minded, up into the obviously irritated face of my instructor and his usual pupil.

Neither returned my smile or made eye contact and I immediately felt a burden to them.

"I'm Vincent," I slowly rose attempting to retrieve the mood a little by extending a hand.

"Hello Vincent," came the curt reply in unison without them taking up my offered hand and ignoring my implied enquiry as to their names.

My heart sank and, for the first time – and I thought I would never say this – I missed Quentin. Apparently he was ill and hence I had been dumped upon the anonymous pair.

Never before, in any situation, had I been made to feel the outsider so much as during the following hours. We split the driving duties so that I did some, then my nameless colleague did some and each time the instructor held up "Golden Boy" – who in fact was as wide as he was tall (5ft!), wore three days of stubble and whose shaved head, like a map of the moon, revealed wide, light-coloured craters where hair no longer grew – as the wonderful example that I should be attempting to emulate.

The criticism was not solely aimed at me – although it must be said that I did bear more than I thought was my fair share – but also at the apparently poor instruction that I had hitherto received from Quentin.

"He told you to do *that!?*" would be the incredulous reply when he questioned my actions and even "micro-thug" joined in with the odd smirk, and "tut".

Initially my confidence was undermined by the pairs' abundance of self-assuredness, but their combined condescending attitude began to harden my opinion. The more this happened, the strangely more defensive I became of the odd man with fish breath that I called *my* instructor.

Suddenly Quentin's enjoyment of belittling me and my driving was forgotten. Somehow an attack on him was an attack on me and I had had enough.

"Okay, that's enough!" I appropriately blurted out, and drew the car to an abrupt stop in the narrow residential street. The car secured (something must have been working because, even angered, I automatically followed the "handbrake, neutral" routine!) I turned to the shocked pair who still avoided my gaze.

"You seem to have some kind of problem with Quentin," I aimed at the instructor, "but I think he's much more professional than you could ever hope to be," I blasted, not quite 100% comfortable with my elevation of "Mr Trout" to King Prawn but determined to retain my solidarity with him.

The car fell silent and I grabbed the opportunity to direct more irritation at baldy in the back. "And you can keep your smart-arse sniggering to yourself because your driving's not too good either. You might want to question your so-called *instructor*," I raised my eyebrows and emphasised the word slowly and sarcastically, "because he's just using you as a stick to beat me with. When it comes to the test you might be sadly disappointed."

His square, jowly face peered silently and open-mouthed back at the instructor's gaze in the rear view mirror for some support but, to my amazement, the car again was still but for the gentle purring of the engine and ticking of the indicator that I had left on.

Then, without moving his gaze from the long line of parked cars in the quiet street before us, the instructor broke the expectant atmosphere. "You have stopped in a less than convenient position here," he sneered. "I think that speaks for itself when we are talking about driving ability doesn't it?" He slowly turned to face me for the first time and his eyes lit faintly with a smile of evil satisfaction.

Boiling again, I wanted to punch his smarmy, tight-lipped grin but retained enough control to refrain from any move that could be terminal for my career before it had begun.

The final trigger was a snort of amusement from the rotund side-kick git on the back seat. If I hadn't had left at that point I don't know what would have happened but I couldn't imagine continuing for the remaining hour of the lesson with these two.

However, even while I was ripping the seatbelt off and swinging my legs out of the open door, beetle-on-his-back-like, to make a swift and furious exit, I realised that my timing was far from ideal.

An hour from the end of the lesson meant that we were probably at the furthest point from the office and I had to find my own way back from where? I hadn't a clue where I was.

In spite of these considerations racing through my mind and colliding chaotically with my bursting anger, I continued my stride away from the abandoned open driver's door without a glance back. I could not let my steps falter for a second at this point. Not until I had heard the, by now, distant clunk of the same door closing and the car moving smoothly away. Not until then did I risk a quick peek over my shoulder to glimpse the car disappear around a bend and into a clutter of parked cars and oncoming traffic. Only now could I relax my unsustainable stride and started to unravel my knotted thoughts enough to plan my long route home.

However, in spite of these frustrating episodes and following my first-time success with the theory test, I soon went confidently onto the driving test proper.

I would have to undergo a full test but, unlike the new learners, I would have to complete all aspects of the syllabus, including every manoeuvre, driving at high speed on a dual carriageway and in difficult, narrow inner-city streets. Additionally, whereas a new learner is allowed 15 minor errors before fail (sorry, are unsuccessful) a trainee driving instructor is allowed only 6 minor faults in the hour-long test. Of course, as with all learners, you are not allowed any major faults.

However, if you make it, you can proudly go by the title of PDI, or Potential Driving Instructor and apply for a pink "triangle" licence which allows you to conduct driving lessons for up to six months, in which time you have to take the dreaded "Part 3" instructional test to become a fully-fledged ADI. An Approved Driving Instructor.

My test was largely uneventful and went well. I passed with just two minor errors, one for not anticipating that a pedestrian was about to step off the kerb and threaten to walk out between two parked vans. It seemed so very much like some Theory Test Hazard Perception video that I have often wondered since whether it was staged?

I gained my second error for leaving my front wheel about two inches further from the kerb than my rear wheel whilst completing a parallel park manoeuvre.

As the examiner took pride in telling me, "The DSA stipulates that I should, *Reverse-park the vehicle into a space behind a parked car within the space of about two car lengths and close to and parallel with the kerb with reasonable accuracy and effective all round observation...*"

He was a nice chap overall, but really should get out a bit more.

**Part 3**

The roles were reversed (excuse the pun!) for some of the following weeks as other pupils were "doubled up" with Quentin and myself during the summer holiday period. We were, however, a little more welcoming to our "outsiders" to say the least and, for the most part, lessons went smoothly, to plan and were almost enjoyable!

Quentin reverted to his familiar type, sarcastically confusing the newbies but I was, by this time, able to laugh at his almost pantomime villainy and thereby put our bemused guests at ease.

As Quentin began to enjoy his "baddy" role more and more, his unnecessary obtuseness in simple situations escalated and the whole lesson became a game of whether we could handle his awkwardness or whether he would win. He knew I had joined the game and that I would eventually give as good as I got and help the other pupil too. Knowing this he seemed to feel that he could relinquish any responsibility for the fragile confidence of the new pupil and allow me to protect them. He was free to express his weirdness without limits.

One poor wretch joined us for the first time one bright July morning for our Part 3 training where Quentin played a learner driver and we had to give him instruction.

The new boy was nominated to act as the qualified instructor for the first half of the lesson whilst I observed from the back seat. Initially the obviously petrified pupil stuttered and stammered his uncertain instructions to a silent Quentin as we crept jerkily through the wide, green leafy avenues of affluent Kingston and Wimbledon.

Gradually, however, Quentin began to develop into everyone's worst nightmare of a "real" learner, seizing upon every minute slip that John, my fellow Part 3 student, had the misfortune to utter. Or rather, as the morning deteriorated for him, mutter.

John:          "Turn left at—"

Quentin:      "What here?" immediately swerving the slow moving car to the left and into a private gravel driveway of a rather grand house where he brought the car to an abrupt, crunching halt inches from the bumper of the shocked owner's Jaguar attempting to leave.

Turning to John he routinely delivered the familiar words: "Out of role" like a child in a playground bringing back to life his war game "killed" friend with a slap on the shoulder and the word "released".

"Now," Quentin – who was back as Quentin the Trainer and no longer Danielle (I don't know why Danielle either but it definitely sounded worryingly more like Danielle than Daniel!) his learner driver from Hell alter-ego – announced satisfied with John's pale, open-mouthed shock. "What did you do wrong there?"

His insincere grin grated with his enjoyment as the loose-jawed John wordlessly grunted and shook his slack, clueless face.

"Well John," Quentin condescended, "you must always tell me *when* you want me to do something before telling me *what* to do. Get it?"

Silence fell in the car.

"No. No clue?" Quentin turned the knife.

"How about telling me *'at the next junction turn left,'* that way I've got a very clear instruction and cannot say that you misled me into making a wrong turn."

Highly pedantic, I thought from my back seat and could see the shock begin to ferment and then boil to anger on John's face at such an absurd detail too. No one would ever do such a ridiculous thing. Even a first lesson learner would know better, but Quentin seemed to be amused and I imagined that this was probably the motivation behind the stunt.

The rising temperature in our car filled the momentary silence, broken only by the apparently, equal fury of the house owner behind the wheel of his British Racing Green Jaguar venting, with all his might, his anger through an elongated blast of the horn.

*

"Out of role" was Quentin's favourite phrase and he used it, unfailingly, to make it clear to us that he was no longer Danielle. I think that Quentin had been doing the job for too long! Without knowing his background he seemed to live for his work and the, sometimes, sadistic enjoyment that he could wring from it.

I can't imagine that a Mrs Prout existed but, if she did, I pitied her. Her life must be one relentless fear of his next humiliation with endless "anorak" information of the latest driving techniques.

"How was work today darling?"

"Great. I reduced a grown man to tears in the morning and then, in the afternoon, another told me that I had destroyed his confidence in his 30 years of driving in just two hours."

"Out of role" however, was only to be used by Quentin. This was his power and no one else was going to use it.

*

Back on the road again, I could feel the tension in the air with John giving little more than the necessary repeated directions to Quentin through gritted teeth and, consequently, Quentin was making more and more deliberate errors.

As John now chose to ignore them, every couple of minutes Quentin would say, "John, tell me to pull over somewhere on the left."

John stared a combination of incredulity and daggers at his trainer for asking him to tell him to pull over and remained silent.

Quentin eventually gave in and drew the car to a halt.

"Parking brake on, and gears into neutral," Quentin would whisper to himself each time he stopped followed by a louder and clearer, "Out of role."

Once stationary Quentin would turn to his pupil and relay the catalogue of John's errors since the previous stop and, despite his attempts to draw John into a discussion (which up until that point had been a dictation) he failed.

John's blank face amply displayed his barely contained contempt.

"Okay, back in role" signified the end of Quentin's lecture and our departure.

I attempted to lighten the leaden atmosphere a little by leaning forward between the two front seats and asking a question of two. My rebuff was instant, typical and comical.

"Could you ask your friend in the back," Quentin announced, "to keep quiet while I'm driving. I'm trying to concentrate on learning." He really believed that he was a learner! At that point his *Am Dram* self had taken over.

I sat, smiling, back in my seat behind, er, Danielle and glanced at John's rear view mirror to catch his smiling eyes and gently shaking head.

Well it worked, I thought to myself as I grinned back. We were back in control of the situation and Quentin had been reduced from an aggravation to a ridiculous amusement.

John visibly relaxed and no longer took the situation seriously. He began to attempt to give instructions and even Quentin's frequent and often petty criticisms failed to deflate him as they had earlier.

We were back on track and the car was a happy one again. Until John's growing confidence crossed the line. Having asked Quentin (sorry Danielle) to pull over just outside the D.I.C.K.S. office near the end of his session, John attempted to ask advice on crossroads and their priorities. A situation we had just encountered with some confusion.

Once fully stopped and having waited for Quentin's whispered instructions to himself to secure the car, John began. "Okay, Quentin. I wasn't sure of the rules back there at the crossroads. Who had the priority in that situation?" A perfectly simple and reasonable question you may have thought.

A short silence marked the end of John's question when a quizzically faced Trainer turned to him and asked, with a straight face, "Who's Quentin?"

Immediately the penny dropped for me but John still looked confused.

"I'm Danielle," Quentin/Danielle explained, "and you're supposed to be my instructor. You shouldn't be asking me those questions should you?"

John smiled at me in his mirror again and thought he knew what he had missed. "Oh, sorry," he conceded but then went on to break the rules big time but uttering Quentin's line. "Out of role please, Quentin."

The magnitude of John's faux pas didn't register with me either, until Quentin, as Danielle, snapped, "Out of role? What does that mean? Do you think I'm playing at driving?"

John joked again in disbelief, "Okay, okay, sorry. But can you please come out of role now?"

Again the reply was of non-comprehension and I saw John's eyes narrow and darken to an angry weariness. "Look Quentin," he spat, "are you going to keep this ridiculous pretence up or are you going to do your job and answer my questions?"

"I don't think an instructor should speak to a pupil like that," Quentin persisted.

"Maybe I should find another one." He pushed too far.

Dumbfounded by Quentin's irrational stubbornness John shook his head in disbelief, turned to me in the back to shake my hand and, ironically, wish me good luck for the afternoon.

The flung, steel seatbelt-catch smacked the door window like a dropped cup on a glass coffee table, the short dark blue car door swung violently open, as if ripped open by a gale onto the narrow pavement and, in one rolling movement, John sprung himself out of his well-crushed bucket seat.

Quentin, still at this point Danielle, looked shocked but had to mumble the words, "Out of role," before allowing himself a mischievous smile and turning to me. "Your turn," he grinned.

What is never usually explained to you when you sign up and hand over the cash for your course is that the, so called, "Part 3" ain't quite as simple as it's portrayed.

"What can be difficult?" you reassure yourself, having whizzed through the Theory test, or "Part 1", and then sailed through the "Part 2" practical driving test.

The big difference is that, whereas with Parts 1 and 2 where you have already gained years of experience and your training has polished you up, no doubt removing one or two dodgy habits picked up over the years, Part 3 is a totally new animal to most of us.

It isn't remotely authentic.

The format:

A Driving Standards Agency examiner (yes you already have a picture of his condescending attitude from behind his clipboard and "Hi-Vis" jacket, don't you!) sits in the driver's seat and pretends to be a learner. The first half hour as a complete beginner and then the second half hour as a pupil approaching their test. You must instruct him at both levels and pass both sections to gain your licence.

Not too bad so far, we've done lots of practice with Quentin "in role" you might think, but the difference here is that the examiner is actively looking for any ambiguity or omissions in your instructions to exploit and magnify 1000%.

You might ask the pupil, "What's the speed limit here?" if they were straying a little above the mark. This is what I had been asked dozens of times during my training and, when the pupil had replied, you either added, "Yes, 30mph, so let's get back to that level" or, if they answered with a teenage, "dunno!" I would tell them, "It's 30mph only, so please check your speedometer and do not exceed it."

On the test, my "pupil" crept over the limit in a 30mph zone, so I started by asking if he knew the speed limit here.

Now, every pupil that I have taught since passing my test has reacted to this question by looking at the speedo and realising that, for me to mention it, they must have been exceeding the limit.

Not so the DSA man. He answered with the stock "Don't know…" and immediately accelerated.

Surprised by this random reaction, I barked that the limit was 30 and that he must not exceed it so he slammed on the brake to bring us down to a creep, quickly creating a confused queue behind us in the high street.

When I finally managed to find a parking space and began to explain that the speed limits were there for a reason and that we were in a busy high street and so people could walk out, etc., etc. – all as per the guide *to good instruction manual* tells us, "Fault Identification, Fault Analysis, Fault Remedy" – my nightmare escalated when he began to yawn, look out of his side window and complain that I was wasting his money being pulled over at the side of the road.

When I told him that I wasn't going to argue with him but it was important to know the rules because of his and others' safety, he jumped on my words as if waiting for them.

"You *are* arguing with me!" he insisted and, when I tried to ignore it and press forward with some instruction to get him moving again, he complained, "Don't just ignore me coz I beat your argument." Goading me into a denial again, which descended into a pantomime, "No I didn't." "Yes you did." episode.

He later claimed, during the post-test debrief, that I had not identified the fault and hence the problem had ballooned.

His fault was that when I told him to stick to the speed limit of 30 I didn't make it clear that that should be miles per hour or kilometres per hour and so, to be safe, he slowed to the kph speed on the speedo.

When I mentioned that there had already been a fault before because he was speeding, he brushed that off with a brief, "Oh, that happens in real life. Concentration slips. Not really a problem was it?"

Real life? I thought, the rest of that afternoon has never before or since happened to me.

There was definitely pressure on the "Part 3" test because, since passing your "Part 2" you are permitted to teach for six months in order to gain practical experience of teaching.

This is called the "Pink" or Trainee licence as opposed to the "Green" which show that you have fully qualified by passing all three tests.

Whilst on the "Pink" you earn a fair wage and, as the Part 3 test approaches, you realise that, should you fail in your three attempts to pass it your income stops there and then AND, to continue, you have to re-start the training right back at the theory stage again. Quite an incentive to pass but also an ingredient to sufficiently add enough pressure to concern the coolest of candidates.

Another little-mentioned fact, when you begin training for your new career, is the Part 3 pass rate for many training establishments!

Needless to say, the D.I.C.K.S. were not the best in the country. Tucked away in the small, small print at the back of one of their many glossy brochures was the shameful figure: 8%.

Yes, just 8%. I looked hard and read it again. Maybe I had read it wrongly. Perhaps only 8% fail or the 7 or 8 before the 8% had not been printed properly.

But no. It definitely said "8%". My heart sank when I read it first.

I was up for my test the following week and this seemed to confirm my suppressed suspicion that maybe I could have chosen better or asked more questions when I signed up.

It felt like expecting a top degree from a university that promised (and charged) for Oxford University standard tuition but revealed, shortly before your finals, that they had equipped you with a GCSE level education.

They, I now realised, were pinning their hopes (and I think that is all they were!) on me, and the many other clueless suckers, to raise their average and along with it their reputation in order to dupe the next generation of lambs.

Nevertheless, the countdown to Part 3 number 1 was on and, in spite of the 8% knock, I felt determined and confident in myself.

\*

The beautiful August afternoon was suddenly clouded by the examiner's words. "I'm afraid that you've not been successful on this occasion." Then adding the smirk slap, "But I think you knew that already."

No, I didn't already know that! In fact I thought I had done well. Done just as I always did with those D.I.C.K.S!

After my initial defeated and greatly deflated feeling however, I gathered myself and found comfort in the fact that it was a marginal fail and that number two would be much better.

During my compulsory extra driving training whilst awaiting my second Part 3 attempt, I continued to follow the instructions of the D.I.C.K.S. "experts" and worked hard at aiming for a good pass this time. Not just a scrape through.

Just three days before my test my usual instructor was unavailable so another took over just for my final hour. Sixty minutes later my confidence had totally evaporated again.

"When's your test?" the new man unnervingly asked.

"Thursday," I chirpily replied.

It's amazing what a slight raise of one eyebrow can do.

Realising the effect of his obvious surprise at my answer he attempted to make amends with, "Ah well, it's worth a try!"

But it was hardly comforting especially as my regular "mentor" had already told me before my *first* test that I was ready.

Needless to say, I did not pass.

My examiner this time, an evil bastard by the name of Bill Kwyette, obviously took pleasure in his perceived power. As his alter-ego pupil, he continually contradicted, argued and used every means possible to distract me from my task, in spite of my attempts to control him by regularly stopping the car and trying to diffuse the artificial (and, to be honest, ridiculously unreal) disagreements.

His verdict at the end was far less gentle, or professional, than his predecessors. "You've failed." He beamed after having left me for 30 minutes alone in the car awaiting the inevitable result. "You're a nice enough person," he grudgingly conceded, "but you have no control of your pupil in the car."

He smirked further as this, I sensed, was the part he enjoyed the most and I wondered how many others he had destroyed that day.

My score was 2-3 meaning that for the first part of the test (the novice learner) I scored two out of six and for the second part, (the pre-test pupil) I achieved only three out of six. In order to pass you need at least four in both sections.

This, after all my extra training, was worse than my first attempt. That time I almost made it with a 3-4.

To say that I was devastated is an understatement. The only redeeming factor was that this was just test two and I still had another one to go.

Test three definitely needed a different approach.

That approach, I decided, did not include any D.I.C.K.S!

By that time I had lost all confidence in their training and my eyes had begun to open to their tactics. Namely:

1   Take as much money from me at the beginning – in my case £2,500.

2   Waffle through some impressive looking brochures whilst I did the theory and driving work.

3   Then, just when I needed some help, drive me around and around in circles for my Part 3 "Training", telling me that I am good, until I fail the test so many times that I give up.

No, I concluded, I needed a fresh angle and so looked to the internet for inspiration. Now I know what you are saying, "Uh oh! Dangerous move." But I was fully aware of the risks involved. Take a chance on a possible cowboy who may fleece me and I fail or, stay with the limp D.I.C.K.S… and fail. With the former, at least, I might be lucky and he may turn out to be genuinely good. The hard part, however, was ploughing through the traffic jam of offers promising to help me *"sail through Part 3"*.

After several days' research, I whittled them down by resisting the *too good to be true* promises made to catch your eye like:

"We can, almost, **GUARANTEE** you a pass!" They didn't inspire too much confidence with their "almost" in spite of the large, bold but ultimately worthless GUARANTEE.

"Don't go for grade 4 when we can get you a grade 6!"

I wasn't choosy at that point. A nice comfortable 4-4 would be fine with me.

"Spend just three weeks with us in County Donegal and you will wonder how you ever failed before."

If it was that simple why did I need three weeks to knock me into shape? After all I did already have the dubious experience of two previous tests.

Apart from the obvious cost of three weeks away from work, the final nail in the coffin for the Irish experience was the tiny small print quoting, "All inclusive course £3,250. Not including accommodation."

My eventual decision fell upon a company who, unfortunately for me based in The South, were located in Hull. Their links popped up everywhere and glowing testimonials, that I was able to check with, from all over the UK, persuaded me that £500 spent with them over two days was an investment worth risking.

Within two hours of meeting Jon, it was like dawn had just broken after the darkest of nights and I already wanted (yes, wanted!) to take the test there and then. No more nerves. The pressure I had felt knowing my job was on the line, evaporated and I could not wait to get started.

I took the one-hour test in Hull and was rewarded with a pass! I had made it and I felt like a kid who had just been picked for the school football team for the first time. My face ached from the grin.

The jovial mood in the car with the examiner was a million miles from the intimidation the previous examiners had enjoyed as he explained that it had been and excellent "lesson" for him and that just one minor omission from me had cost me a grade six. The top score.

Fully chuffed (and mightily relieved!) I called The D.I.C.K.S. office but my gabbled good news was initially met with silence. Then the incredulous man's voice slowly and calmly repeated my words to him.

"You, passed?" he added as confirmation for himself and, I imagine, for his open-mouthed colleagues sitting within earshot of his desk, "and you got a grade five?" he went on, prompting me for a reiteration which I gladly delivered.

However, at this point I became slightly uneasy by his apparent tone of disbelief and he seemed to pick up on my frustration because his voice changed and he cheerfully congratulated me and added, "You better get yourself in here with your paperwork then and we can get you a job."

"We guarantee you a job when you have finished training" the D.I.C.K.S. proudly repeated many times during my time there so I naturally thought, Well, that can't be a con too... Can it?

To be fair, no, it isn't a con. Just not what I expected!

On my final return to the appropriately abbreviated training establishment, I was handed one faxed A4 sheet of paper.

"Your job guarantee," the grinning tutor smirked, knowing exactly what I was thinking, but not giving a toss.

The sheet contained approximately 30 contact names and telephone numbers of Driving Schools, ranging from the big national names to the one man bands, in the area I had chosen to teach.

As if to ratchet up the insult he lethargically mumbled, "You can use the pay-phone in the hallway," as he strolled from the classroom.

Disbelief boiled to anger then cooled to a kind of, *Well what did I really expect?* attitude as I gathered my papers and, deflated, slowly filed from the flimsy hardboard and frosted glass partitioned cell.

I didn't take up the generous pay phone offer, preferring the *mobile phone when I get home* option.

## Chapter 2 – The Con Continued

My wife and I had decided, having battled my way through South West London's choked roads and against their, shall we say, less than considerate drivers, that once qualified, we would take my new portable career to the fresh air and coastline of southern England. An ideal spot, not too far from friends and family, but far enough away to breathe and slow our pace of life a little. Well, that was the theory before we moved anyway.

Having scanned the list for my chosen area I discovered that, of the thirty or so names on offer, only five were within ten miles of my home, the rest being as far afield as Southampton or Salisbury or Yeovil or Bristol!

Living in Godskerk and working in Bristol? Mmmm, could enlarge my, already, expanding carbon footprint, turning it from green to red.

So, five phone calls.

Four answer machines.

One answer.

Their enthusiasm to accept an untried rookie stunned me but they couldn't wait to sign me up and I felt chuffed that I had landed a job at the first attempt. Never once did it occur to me that this was too good to be true. That there might be a catch.

No, with my naïve smugness I played it cool and told them that I was considering several other offers and would let them know as soon as I had decided.

"Okay," the smiling and knowing female voice at the other end replied, "looking forward to seeing you soon then."

A bit arrogant and overconfident, I thought to myself.

A week later, having had no reply to my other four phone calls despite chasing them up, I spoke to the lady again. I explained to her that, after careful consideration, her offer was the best and I could tell from her practised replies that I was not the first to have this awkwardly false conversation with her as we set a date to meet in the office to sign me up. I could almost hear her saying to her colleagues when she had hung up, "Ah, bless. He thinks I believe him."

"Welcome to The PAs" the small, shabbily suited young man grinned. *The* Pass Accelerators, as they arrogantly referred to themselves, was embodied before me by the skinny, pale "boy" as he extended his grey bony fingers toward me in greeting. Instinctively I grasped his hand which instantly dissolved into all the characteristics of an empty rubber glove as it was withdrawn rather too quickly to signify genuineness.

"Firstly, I would like to present you our front desk team." He hurried on in his best *I am a serious businessman* voice and motioned with his right arm to the one occupied desk behind us.

My guide, whose name had yet to be announced, smiled proudly at a tall, dark-haired woman hunched busily over an old green and black PC screen and two telephones, one of which was lying "open" on the desk, the other pressed to her ear. Feeling our gaze upon her, she waved her free hand briefly and raised her head in a reverse nod by way of acknowledgement before returning her attention to her phone call and dusty screen. She was the "Front Desk Team"!

Even my host felt the awkwardness of his own over exaggeration feeling the need to qualify the situation with, "Normally she's not alone of course. Sickness and holidays you know!" he tutted and raised his eyebrows.

At that moment, his own phone rang and, although he attempted to ignore it, it, along with several pointed glances from "The Team", forced him into action. "Good-er-morning to you! You are through to *The* P.As. in Weychester and my name is Seamus. How can I possibly help you this-er-morning?" he stumbled toward the end realising repetition and looked, slightly red-faced in my direction.

Heaven help us! I thought to myself. This is surely a sit-com.

The one side of the conversation that I could hear indicated that Seamus had been lucky enough to pick up a complaint. In fact, judging by his long silences interrupted only by the occasional "But er…" or "well Madam if I can…" he was on the end of a rant.

His hollow cheeks that seemed never to have yet needed a razor, reddened further as he listened and continued to glance sheepishly at me and raising his eyebrows again. This time apparently mocking the unstoppable caller he even pointed and silently laughed at the angry receiver for my benefit.

"Okay Madam," he finally managed, "I will fully investigate and report back to you as soon as possible but I'm glad you understand our point of view too."

My interest focussed along with that of "The Team".

"However, in future, please don't use that tone with me or my staff again" (his colleague looked daggers from her desk at the mention of "my staff") "or we will have to withdraw our service from your son."

Questions immediately surfaced.

How could she understand his point of view?

This was the first complete sentence he had been able to utter.

How had he suddenly asserted himself in the conversation having struggled throughout?

Suspicions arose within me that the caller had long since hung up and that Seamus' controlled summary may just have been for my benefit. Suspicions reinforced by "The Team's" sniggering shake of her head.

"Some people just don't understand the complications of this industry," he continued. "Now er, what was your name again?" he asked but continued without looking up from his chaos of paperwork, "where were we? Ah yes," my host went on with what appeared to be, a well-practised monologue whilst he presented me with an ill-shuffled pile of dog-eared A4 forms. "Once you've read and signed your life away," he snorted at his wit, "let me know and we'll meet..." he made the inverted commas sign, with his index and middle fingers of both hands, either side of his head and slowly and deliberately mouthed "...the big boss."

I was wrong.

This wasn't a sit-com.

It was a pantomime!

"Okay, do you have a pen?" I innocently enquired.

"Oooo," Seamus was off balance for a moment, "ooo-er-well, yes," he eventually conceded as he slapped his ribs through his limp jacket in a fruitless search, before snatching one from his colleague's desk. "However," his tone dropped to an unconvincing seriousness, "This is a team pen," he said as he held the chewed and non-descript biro directly in front of my face, "and as such must be returned to the team desk immediately after you finish."

My open mouth rendered me speechless as Seamus continued to apparently quote from the company rulebook, "The PAs do not supply instructors with ancillary equipment and therefore, in future, it is your responsibility to provide what is necessary to effectively carry out your work."

No, wrong again.

Not even a pantomime.

Just a farce.

"This is Vincent," Seamus announced from outside the open door of what appeared to have once been a walk-in wardrobe and, walking backwards and bowing almost reverently, slipped, Baldrick-like, back along the dark corridor.

"Come in…" a slow voice beckoned me in, accompanied by another outstretched hand. This time, the hand rose disinterestedly from a seated position from behind a desk that almost filled the room. "…er, er, Vincent?" he questioned.

Already I felt too minor a matter for him but nevertheless introduced myself. "Hello" was my feeble start as I looked in vain for a seat, although I could see that my host was reclined in a high-backed leather-look executive beast which would be at home in the office of a multi national CEO. In this dim-lit cupboard, however, it served only to expose its occupant's delusions and to fill the remaining few square inches of the room.

"My name is Mike," he started, "and, on behalf of The PAs, I would like to welcome you aboard and assure you that we pride ourselves on the quality of our service and that we are at the forefront of innovations within the driving instruction industry."

He greeted me as he aimlessly shuffled my forms delivered by his sidekick, looking only at the signature on the back page.

The words then began to blur as I sniffed another well-rehearsed script and I tried to hide my half laugh with a false yawn, thought better of it as it was my first day and developed it further into a much more acceptable false sneeze.

Yes, a money making machine I'm sure but "innovative" and an "industry" it could hardly be used to describe it! Even I, as "green" as I was standing in that office for the first time, could see that. Far too shambolic. As for it being at the "forefront" of anything, well maybe only with premium prices charged to both its pupils and to a large number of its instructors who have yet to fully qualify, and even for some who indeed would eventually never qualify! Now, I might, at a stretch and if I were an estate agent, describe this as an "entrepreneurial opportunity" however other, less kind words, more immediately spring to mind!

The regurgitated blurb continued as my mind further wandered to the dark cork-tiled walls of the windowless office and to the many and varied scraps of wilting and yellowed newspaper cuttings, Excel graphs and well-thumbed Indian, Pizza and Chinese restaurant menus pinned chaotically to them.

My numb daydream broke suddenly and sharply with the matter-of-fact words, "£345 per week" whilst Mike skimmed onto "and you will receive a fully liveried car approximately every six months."

"What was that about £345 per week?" I blurted, disbelievingly out, disappointed at a wage that was far less than the £550 to £575 I had been lead to believe I could earn by the D.I.C.K.S. "Just £345?" I stopped Mike mid-flow.

"Yes," the large, round, shiny face that now leant forward and appeared through the brown light of the room and relaxed to a faint smile. "Yes, that's all," he continued, "and I must say that you are first person to say that to me and I am pleased that you understand that our business plan is the best to develop you career." He snorted a grunt-like laugh, "Car-eer, geddit?"

I did, and smiled back sympathetically.

The brief genuine light in his demeanour quickly faded and he returned to the well-trodden company line with, "Because, remember, your business is our business and our business is for you."

I attempted to ignore the rising nausea at the sales-speak and returned to my question: "No," I insisted, "I don't think you understand. I thought I'd be earning much more than £345 a week. My trainers told me average earnings are much more."

The shiny, round face, dulled and lengthened as it retreated back into the dimness and let the smile fall from it. "No," he contradicted as his voice softened, "I'm afraid *you* haven't understood."

He cleared his throat before delivering the blow. "You pay *us* £345 per week."

The claustrophobic cube-room fell silent at his shocking clarification.

Mike's telling embarrassed awkwardness forced him to break the shivering stillness. "It's our franchise fee," his voice was noticeably weaker than before, but gained confidence again as he continued, "but for that you get the full office back-up of our Front Desk Team," worth all of a fiver I thought to myself, "a new car every six months," he repeated grasping desperately, "no service or repair costs," his justification weakened further.

"Diesel?" I optimistically helped out looking for some light.

"Er, no," he stumbled again, "not fuel, but," he tried again, "you will carry the badge of the best known, most respected and longest serving instruction business in the world." His pitch finally and weakly dried up and I was still too shell-shocked to fully respond.

The questions in my head rose to a crescendo – *£345 per week. How could I afford that? How much would I get after all that was taken off? And fuel on top!*

I felt sick, but the reality dawned that I had no other offers. No alternative and if I had, they would probably be just as expensive. My whole career choice suddenly seemed to be a con.

I had fallen for the TV adverts, the, now even more appropriately named, D.I.C.K.S.' sales banter. I had laughed at their name then but they'd been laughing at me all the time too, and now seemed to have the last laugh after their sub-standard instruction. I even had to pay out more to get myself through the Part 3 test. Now, just when I thought I'd start to earn something back instead of constantly pay out, I was being fleeced again!

My initial excitement at being "accepted" by the, so-called, best, The PAs, at my first attempt instantly drained away along with the contents of my bank account.

My eyes were finally fully opened to driving instruction. I, along with the unsuspecting teenage pupils and their parents, was a customer. Not an employee as the learners saw me. Just another regular pay-cheque for The PAs. They had built an excellent business model. Have as few employees as possible (i.e. The Front Desk Team), make it appear, however, to the public that your company employs a large number of instructors by accepting every Potential Driving Instructor (PDI) – partly trained instructor – that contacts you and charge everyone a top rate for the well-known brand. They even produce their own customers through their instructor training programme whilst charging them to train before, yes you've guessed it, charging them to work.

Finally, to add insult to injury, there was little interest in whether their PDIs passed or failed their final exams because there was always a supply of new "victims" waiting in the wings to be "trained".

I was trapped and Mike, for all his embarrassment, knew it. I felt angry, foolish and naïve but there was no turning back now. I was going to have to work at it.

## Chapter 3 – A Lesson... For Everyone

### Lessons

I stood awkwardly upright facing the white uPVC and frosted glass door, my heart off-beating like a fired pinball as the sweet, lazy two-tone of the doorbell melted into the corridor behind. Almost two years' training had come to this moment. Two years in which my driving skill and thus, as a man my pride, had been shredded, panel-beaten and re-assembled by cowboys. Two years of frequent humiliation by trainers, half my age, telling me in rather blunt terms, that my driving was seriously lacking.

At times, in fact during most of the time, I had hated it, despised it and, after each gruelling three-hour lesson, I had been relieved to get on a bus home, mightily disinclined to return and intimidated by the frighteningly high standard expected of me when I finally qualified. What kind of polished excellence was being demanded out there by the pupils?

But right this moment, as the watery shadow began to fade into view through the rippled pane, I would have gladly gone back to the training's miserable familiarity, its compromised cosiness, rather than start my first lesson.

The shadow indecisively grew and faded on the other side of the door like a nervous goldfish in a fairground plastic bag and I felt my cheery welcome smile fix and begin to ache in my jaw.

Richard himself, stood 6' 2" tall, was built like the proverbial, but acted and spoke like one far older than his tender 17 years. Throughout his considerable time with me, Richard remained a partial puzzle. What I did glean from him over time was that he was the youngest (by a long way) of four boys and that his wealthy family lived in Suffolk in, from his snippets of description, an extremely large home on their estate. Mum and Dad appeared to have retired but had previously had long, successful and powerful careers in the city. As what, alas, remained shrouded.

Every sentence ended with the intonation up, like that of a question (or of a cast member of *Neighbours*) and, from his years of apparent parental over-encouragement and support as the baby of the family, he believed 110% in his own abilities, whether or not they existed, taking every compliment from me for his "start, stop, hop, stall" driving of the first months, to further endorse and inflate his, on first glance, cast-iron ego. I say, "on first glance" because the oddest of things would suddenly throw him off course. Things that one would not imagine could shake his solid belief in himself could drastically affect him.

After several months of lessons Richard was now moving the car from A to B without stalling, working up and down through the gears and sometimes not even hitting the kerb when he parked!

He was happy. I was happy.

Until, that is, a well-intentioned courtesy call from one of the girls (sorry, *the* girl) on The PA's "Front Desk Team" gave me the first glimpse of Richard's fragility. The call was only to ask if he had thought to book his theory test in order that it would not hinder his progress toward the practical driving test. If not, then the office staff would routinely book the test for the pupil themselves.

Quite often pupils get so advanced with their driving that they forget that they have to pass the theory test before they move onto the practical test. At that point some of those who have already had a belly full of recent GCSEs or A Level exams are loathed to revise for yet another hurdle and find that they take it too lightly, assuming that it is just a formality.

This is where things begin to falter.

They are ready for their practical driving test and they want to take it as soon as possible because financial pressure means that they cannot afford to continue lessons ad infinitum on the basic wage they receive from working evenings in Tesco. So reluctantly they book and pay, the not inconsiderable sum, for their theory test. But they do not put the necessary hours of revision in, because they feel they already know what they are doing after some months of driving. They cannot afford to spend the extra money on revision books and the time that the test needs because of school, work and leisure and finally because of the attitude, "if that loser 'Jonny' at school can do it first time, so can I."

Yes, you guessed it.

They fail.

Then they try again, convinced that they were either, unlucky, "I just failed by one mark!" (how many times have I heard that?!) or nervous or that they were the victims of some conspiracy to keep the number of young drivers off the road.

They fail again.

Then they get annoyed, embarrassed, impatient. Anything but motivated to do it properly next time. Quite possibly they fail again and in the meantime they have reduced their lessons to once every two weeks instead of weekly, or worse still to one hour a week, most of which is spent getting to and from the test area to practise.

The consequence is that their driving standard falls through lack of practice, declining concentration and finally loss of interest. Then they disappear, blaming the system for their very expensive failure (all very British) only to finally re-surface some years later as those self-confessed "late starters" who tell you of their teenage driving flops.

Anyway, back to Richard.

Following the phone call, Richard did not understand that it was designed to minimise his cost and maximise the efficiency of the lessons. He felt only the pressure from the young girl's voice at the other end pushing him into somewhere he didn't want to go. Where a simple "No thanks" would have sufficed, Richard just hung up in a blind panic.

His father later called me warning that it was unacceptable that I should pressure him in such a manner and told me that he felt unable to take his next two lessons because of the upset.

He wasn't the only upset one now, I thought. I was also stunned, firstly because until that point I had known nothing of the courtesy call and secondly this did not sound like the Richard I knew.

Many months later, when the subject re-arose, his dad explained that Richard, if I hadn't by now already have worked it out, was full of, what I shall call here, bluff. As long as he felt in control of the situation he was okay, but the bravado soon evaporated the moment that control seemed to have been relinquished.

I had learned an important lesson in how to handle a delicate character like Richard and eventually felt lucky not to have inadvertently upset him before. Nevertheless the old Richard was back with me two weeks later, insisting that he knew all his theory, knew the spec and performance of every sports car that passed us and really knew how to drive quite well. All he believed he needed were a few more lessons to hone his skills.

I suddenly began to dread having to introduce the mandatory manoeuvres!

When I finally did bite the bullet the results were, well, mixed and eventful. Just reversing in a short, straight line proved a challenge as I tried to explain how "reference points" worked (i.e. fix a point on the window through which you are looking and keep the car relative to that point throughout the manoeuvre and you should remain in the correct position). During the straight line reverse this point is often the point at which the kerb behind us appears to dissect a point approximately in the middle of the rear window.

Richard, having required several different approaches by me to understand the concept, finally grasped it on the fourth explanation and instantly became impatient at my further efforts to check that he fully understood.

"Yes, yes," he sighed, "shall we try it then?"

Resigned to his sudden rush, I agreed and, at great speed we lurched backwards, rode up upon the kerb and only failed to hit a lamppost by my using the dual-control footbrake.

"There's something wrong with the clutch," Richard announced. "It sprung up too quickly. You should get that seen to, it's dangerous."

I bit my lip… very hard. We moved forward to the starting position again and recomposed ourselves.

"Right, Richard, have you found a reference point?" I asked, half expecting a *"Der! Yeah of course"* but instead received just a teenage grunt.

"Where is it then?" I explored further.

"On the end of the sticker," he grudgingly confirmed.

"Okay, I am going to let us move slowly backwards and I want you to keep a firm eye on that point, not letting the kerb move from it for a second."

I tried to consolidate the instructions with "If it begins to move, re-adjust the steering wheel to get us back on track. Do you understand?" I enquired.

A long, deep *I'm bored* sigh was followed by "Mmmmmm."

As we, this time, crept slowly backwards I watched as Richard stared, unblinkingly at the spot he had set himself on the rear windscreen.

"Is the kerb still on the reference point?" I asked.

"Yeah," he huffed, momentarily breaking from his trance and uncrossing his eyes.

However, as we continued to progress along the road it became clear that we were gradually edging toward the kerb, so I asked as to the position of the reference point only to receive an irritated "Yessss" from very close range.

Unfortunately, as you are peering over your left shoulder, whilst the car rolls backwards, if you move your head too much you can manipulate the point and the accuracy is lost. In other words you either hit the kerb or drift out into the middle of the road.

As we had moved, Richard had indeed leaned further and further toward me in an attempt to compensate for the shifting reference point instead of adjusting the steering. Naturally, having stopped with our nearside rear wheel firmly on the pavement, Richard confidently announced that there was either something wrong with the steering or the reference point method clearly did not work.

Despite these hurdles however, after quiet and persistent insistence on my behalf that the fault lay not with the tools but with the "craftsman" (or in this case "the apprentice") Richard mastered the straight line reverse, typically rounding off the exercise with, "I'm pretty good at that I think."

No need for praise from me then.

His confidence re-inflated like never before, I mischievously decided to push him a little further before the end of the lesson.

"Okay Richard," I said, "having done such a good job on the straight line, let's try to reverse around that corner." I pointed ahead of our parked position to a side road on the left.

Richard's brow furrowed and I could feel the advent of more wise words from an old-fashioned head on young shoulders.

"Do you think that wise?" was the slightly condescending tone.

Surprised by the question I began to think that he thought that I was pushing him too far in one lesson. I tried, therefore, to explain. "Well, it's quite similar to the straight line you just did and I will guide you through each step of the turn."

"No, no," he smirked at my misunderstanding, closing his eyes as he explained, "that's not the problem, it just seems rather dangerous."

"Why?" I asked, even more confused.

"Because it's at a junction." Became the, *well isn't it obvious*, reply.

A short silence fell in the car as I fathomed his logic and then asked, "Where else can we reverse around a corner?" Another silence descended as he registered his error but, refused to allow it to dent his belief or lead to any embarrassment.

"You might be right on this occasion," he merely conceded.

Almost beaten by the irritation heating up inside me, I called it a day and Richard drove home.

*

Oliver was strange.

Even from when I first knocked at his door for our first lesson I sensed the vibes were odd. I could see him approach the partially glazed door, then duck down and tiptoe away before he thought he had been spotted.

Then another, shorter shadow strode purposefully toward the door and whipped it open smartly. It was mum, wearing one bright-yellow left Marigold which was strangling the right one like a skinny, limp and plucked chicken. Her face was rushed red and wore a temporary and transparent smile. A poor fit to cover her agitation, the cause of which stood arched behind her like a crane over a small building.

"You're here for Oliver?" she breathlessly enquired before I could speak and stepped back to open the door wider to allow the reluctant shadow to come into full focus.

Emerging from the white, kitchen light behind him, Oliver resembled the silhouetted aliens we see gliding from the glow of their gleaming spaceships, until the towering frame – for that is what he was! – filled the doorway that he stooped to exit.

Oliver, at 17 years old, must have been 6'4" was built like a pipe cleaner and walked with the flop of an excited Alsatian puppy. His endless, skin-tight jeans resembled two blue scaffold tubes and his soft-looking grey and white hooped hoodie sleeves were pushed up to the elbows to disguise their inability to reach his distant wrists.

"'wight?" he nodded.

My heart slowed as it sank. Before me stood the living version of the silk-like, man-shaped wind socks seen at fairgrounds and "massive tyre sales", that contort, twist and writhe to the constant air blasted through them.

Oliver's first challenge presented itself as I held open the driver's door of my gleaming new, orange stickered Vauxhall Corsa. Ushering my first pupil into his seat like a hotel porter returning a valet-parked car.

Is it left leg or right leg first?

He shuffled, half crouched to duck his head in, swapped standing legs frequently whilst deciding his approach, then finally concluded that the best way was to dive head-long through the opening, drawing his telescopic legs in behind him.

From my perspective, still holding his door, it made an amusing spectacle as the car seemed to swallow him whole like some bulbous amber and grey anaconda. Having folded himself into an origami frog behind the steering wheel, Oliver turned his nervously smiling face to me in a visible sense of achievement.

Now he was ready to take on the road.

My mouth still open, I gently closed the door. Once in my seat I tried to veil my amazement at the level of difficulty my pupil had introduced to the simple task of his entry and wondered at the lessons that lay ahead for him. And me!

The formalities completed, driving licence checked, a few forms completed and, of course the compulsory eye test joke – "Now Oliver, can you read the number plate of that car please?"

"What car?" – followed by a crisp snapping sound as my uncontrollable laughter broke my ribs one by one, we got down to some serious tuition.

Namely the so-called "Cockpit Drill". A grand name for the routine checks to set the seat and mirrors etc. before starting the car up.

All went well as Oliver followed my instructions in order, making sure his door was secure and his seat and steering wheel were set correctly but when we reached his seatbelt, challenge number two became apparent. Now, to be fair to Oliver, this was the first time I had seen such a performance, but I have, on a very few occasions, seen it since, so he is not alone. Nevertheless it never fails to puzzle me how such a simple move can be made so complicated.

On my instruction, Oliver grasped the shiny silver tongue of the belt, hanging just above and behind his right shoulder, between his left forefinger and thumb. So far so good, until he then pulled the belt over his head so that the top half was behind his neck and the bottom half across his chest!

His right hand then took the grasp and completed the move by plugging the metallic buckle into the latch on the stalk beside his left hip. From this position he wriggled his neck and shoulders, Houdini-style, out from under their constraint to finally place the belt in its correct position across his chest and lap. However, in negotiating this intricate manoeuvre, Oliver had managed to twist the belt and, as this could prove dangerous in an accident, I pointed this out to him, asking him to unwind it.

This, for my new, enthusiastic friend, was easier said than done. I watched mesmerised for what seemed like minutes as the, almost flat-pack folded, pupil struggled to iron out the kink in the strap. Firstly he pushed the twist all the way down across his chest to the buckle catch, but it got stuck there. Then he eased it up to his right shoulder and to the loop on the door-post, from which the belt is hung and seemed pleased to leave it there until he loosened his grip and the twist re-appeared across his chest.

His eyes were then temporarily confused until inspiration relit them with the realisation of the obvious and he snorted an embarrassed huff. If he forced the twist through the door-post loop it would stay there and not come back to haunt him!

I allowed this folly to continue for a second or two, his rubber-like upper body contorting whilst both hands struggled and tugged at his stubborn tormentor and his eyes crossed trying to focus closely over his right shoulder before I offered him the, apparently less obvious "unbuckle, untwist, and re-secure" option.

He accepted my advice in his stride (and in silence) then sat back grinning at his successes so far and in anticipation of more.

In spite of this apparent self-satisfaction with small triumphs Oliver never allowed his ego to overwhelm him. In fact, apart from the occasional grin, conversation remained an insurmountable hurdle for him.

In my attempts to lighten the mood of lessons throughout the following weeks, I tried every approach.

"Make the pupil feel as relaxed as possible in this new situation for them," my instructor trainers continually told me.

"Find an interest of theirs and mention it at suitable breaks in the driving."

Well I searched... And searched... and searched but, save for a few rare sparks of contact and bursts of conversation, failed to connect with the mono-syllabic and thus, fleetingly, sinisterly impenetrable Oliver.

"Did you watch the England match last night?"

Greeted with just a sniff and half smile as he, unblinkingly, watched a train blur across the level crossing before us.

I took this as a no, and possibly an impatient one, so I dropped the sport angle. Several minutes later I tried again. This time with school. Maybe there was a clue to his interests from his subjects.

"What are you studying at college?"

"Physics, Maths and Photography," came the promising reply.

"Wow," I enthused, "photography must be interesting."

But surprisingly no reply emerged.

"What do you get to shoot?" I tried again, "Page three stuff?" I snorted, immediately cringing at my, old man trying to sound funny to a teenager, attempt.

But Oliver smiled lightly and at first I thought I'd got away with it. Until the smile continued and its lightness took on the fixed intensity of the Mona Lisa's and his eyes shrank me to an insignificance.

I retreated back to the driving talk for the remainder of the lesson, between which yawned heavy silences that I dared not interrupt. My voice level even faded significantly as my questions took on an increasingly apologetic tone.

Except for a few random replies and inappropriately timed splashes of disarticulated interest and like, after eight, two-hour lessons, he slowly and deliberately unwrapped and unfolded a small pair of metal-framed glasses and brightly announced, "Mmm. I can see much better now," never did I reach a recognisable teenager in Oliver.

# Chapter 4 – Unexpected bumps en route

Luckily for me Oliver seemed to be an exception and I didn't really find myself scared of any other pupils although the random quality of some of them has, on more than one occasion, wrong-footed me.

Several months into my sentence, sorry, career with The PAs and I had enough pupils to keep me "ticking over" but was still far short of the number needed to earn a living. The PAs were paying me the amount I'd earned with one hand but taking it away again with the other, as their ridiculously expensive franchise fee. But, without the contractual option to leave just yet, I looked upon this time as an extension of my training. A kind of half-way house to a job next year. I therefore eagerly (yes, at this point I was still eager!) snapped up any pupils sent my way.

However, one of the major pitfalls of being self-employed in any line of business is being let down at the last minute by customers who have no consideration for, or understanding of, the fact that if I didn't teach then I wouldn't get paid. Worse still, nevertheless I was still charged my franchise fee! Not to mention the diesel, the wasted time, etc., etc.

One solution offered by The PAs was to tell pupils that they would still be charged for a lesson if they cancelled within 48 hours. The drawback there was that, once caught by this clause, they don't turn up for any further lessons and would find another of the numerous independent driving instructors who promised not to charge them in a similar situation.

So I had to weigh up whether occasionally losing £20 for one hour's lesson would be better than potentially losing their business entirely, but then also setting a precedent that they would casually use again in the future!

Getting the pupil to pay in advance by offering a discount was also suggested but again I found that if I took the payment for the missed lesson an outraged parent (suddenly the "all grown up" teenagers needed Mum to speak for them as they stood, towering and stooped, "Rodney-like" behind them) would either demand a refund for the remaining lessons or, come the end of the block booking, they would disappear. Either way would I lose!

So, trying to be fair and hoping that being upfront with them would ease any future situation, I would explain on the first lesson that if they cancelled within 24 hours I would charge them half of the missed lesson's fee... unless there was a seriously good reason for their late withdrawal.

This last concession was a big mistake as you will see from some of the interesting and creative "reasons" I experienced.

"Bring!"

It's Sunday afternoon and my mobile phone's familiar text alert begins its busiest evening.

**"Hi. Can't do my nxt lesson. Soz. Cya nxt time."**

My initial resigned irritation to this familiar saga each week was further prodded each time they omitted to include their name. I know I could have put their names in my phone's contacts but sometimes, with 30 plus pupils, some lasting no more than a couple of weeks and others changing numbers every other week, I never bothered to keep updating my mobile. Hence my partially self-induced frustration as I always had to look through a printed list to discover the sender.

However, sometimes the repeated cheery sparkle of the incoming text alert proved a little too aggravating and my reply would be a somewhat prickly and curt, "Who are you?"

When, after a lengthy pause (during which time I had looked up their number anyway) the mystery pupil had revealed themselves, their tone, no doubt sensing from my brevity my annoyance, had become a little more genuinely apologetic and explained further, "Soz. It's Lee. I gt sum hmwrk 2 do tht I 4got".

Now this may seem a weak excuse for cancelling a one-hour lesson for the next afternoon but, as they go, it was one of the better ones.

"I'm in grease" was one simple explanation and, whilst it diverted my anger and conjured up a number of scenarios ranging from the chorus line of a West End show to a barrel of black engine lubricant, I hoped that they were just on holiday and that their geography was better than their English.

Nevertheless, once the humour of the (il)literacy had worn off, I *did* wonder how quite a major event on their calendar had crept up upon them so unexpectedly as to necessitate a text to me just 20 hours before the lesson. And even what had finally prompted their memory into thinking of a driving lesson whilst snoozing on the beach?

More irritating "reasons" ranged from the vacuous, "I ate my lesson money" from which I guessed that they had spent the money on lunch rather than actually chewed and swallowed two tenners – but you never know, to the ridiculous, "I was 2 drunk to gt hme lst nite so I dnt knw where I am".

Probably to their disappointment I didn't dig for any further clarification but accepted all these along with the catalogue of other "genuine and seriously good" reasons for cancellations.

One classic trilogy of excuses began apparently genuinely enough with one of the pale and frail looking girls texting that she had to cancel because of "heavy period". Too much information to give to your driving instructor of just two lessons so far, I thought, but at least a reasonable postponement.

However, a week later she again texted to cancel, this time with another over descriptive, "**Can't sit dwn 2 long. Ovaries are aking**"

I feared to ask any further questions and so confirmed that I would see her the following week.

Yes. You guessed it already.

About three hours before I was due to pick her up for the next lesson I heard the familiar "coins down a drain" tinkle of an incoming text.

"**The tablets I tk 4 my aking ovaries make me drowsy so cant drive agen.**"

This time I immediately texted back that I would have to charge her for half the lesson as she had cancelled so late.

Her reaction surprised me from such an apparently shy, delicate, fragile creature.

"**Y r u chrgin me? Its not my fault the doc gv me these pills**". She went on, "**I only cnxld l8 coz I 4got the lesson. If u hd remnded me ystrdy then I cud hv dun it earlier**".

Not wishing to be drawn into a "tit for tat texting" I did not reply although my mobile later announced directly, "**I won't be using you again**". I smiled at the irony of her unconscious admission and promise.

However, these were in the minority and, if the truth were known, would probably have turned into "problem" pupils anyway so, in an irritating way, they possibly did me a favour by cutting our relationship short. Some other poor bugger would have to deal with them at a later date!

Most, though, were excited to get driving and looked forward to their lessons.

As a first pupil, Richard did prove a bit of a challenge, but he was reliable and, along with many of his peers, provided some interesting moments.

# Chapter 5 – Signs of Success?

"How much?" I blurted, unable to control my excitement.

"£70 per week," the man's deep voice at the other end of the phone confirmed.

"Wow, that's great. When can I start?" I enthused.

I had completed my minimum one-year term with The PAs the day before and the franchise fee that had just been quoted to me was approximately 20% of that I was paying currently. Admittedly I had to supply my own car but a new Corsa could be leased for about £60 to £70 per week, leaving me quids in!

At last, I thought, I can earn some money. Maybe the "be your own boss and earn £30k" TV adverts were true after all.

I rediscovered the excitement and hope of my first days with The PAs and could not wait to get to work with "NOVICEnoMORE" . Especially as they promised me at least 30 pupils in the first year. This figure was about 30% more that I had received from The PAs who, in a feeble attempt to keep me with them, firstly offered me a £20 reduction in my franchise fee – per month!

Then they tried the flattery angle by claiming that I was "one of their best" (they didn't specify exactly what, but feel free to insert any of the following – suckers, mugs, fools etc.) and that their reputation in Weychester had been greatly enhanced since I had joined the company.

Yeah, right!

Finally, and desperately, they revealed a little of their true colours by trying to rubbish NOVICEnoMORE.

Having successfully resisted their half-hearted attempts to retain their customer (because I knew full well that that was all I was to them) I rushed to the "NOVICEnoMORE" office to sign on the dotted line.

I was greeted by a short, dark-haired young man in a blue suit which seemed to be straining under the almost visible expansion of its owner/occupier. However, my host was pleasant enough, was professional and, refreshingly, seemed genuine too!

He filled several white "NnoM" logoed polythene shopping bags with appointment cards, pre-printed adverts, posters and flyers, business cards and pupil progress reports.

I was impressed! What a difference from the "Here's your car. Get on with it" attitude of The PAs.

Finally, as I was leaving the office, I was presented with a 1m tall cardboard tube. My puzzled look betrayed me and the young expanding man immediately explained.

"Our logos for your car."

It had been mentioned in passing (no pun intended!) that, as part of the franchise agreement it was required of me to "clearly display and maintain" the supplied logos on my car. This, it was explained, was for the benefit of all drivers as, for example, if someone saw the livery on the side of a car passing through my area, they may call us and I would gain a pupil by another driver carrying the logo.

It was then, they argued, only fair that everyone enjoys the same chance of such a windfall and thus all cars were required to carry the logos from day one of their franchise. I understood and didn't see a problem, so I happily accepted my merchandise and looked forward to my career really taking off this time.

"Clean the car surface thoroughly and dry completely – keep out of direct sunlight," I read out loud to myself.

Sounded simple enough so I tipped the oversized toilet roll tube up and out slid a few sheets of bright yellow letters, backed with opaque paper. Then a few more dropped out. And, as I gently shook the tube, even more large capital letters flopped onto the garage floor… followed by a few smaller, mirror written strips of text and numbers. Then some more signs and logos.

The tube, I thought, must have been related to the Tardis but eventually, after one final sheet of "Application Instructions" floated to the ground, the tube was empty.

I must admit that I was surprised by the number of stickers and transfers as I had seen many other NOVICEnoMORE cars on the road sporting only the bare minimum. Namely the name on the doors.

A phone call later, to ascertain as to whether I had received more that I needed, and I understood the volume. For the last month or so NOVICEnoMORE, or NnoM as they now called themselves, had written into their franchise agreements that "all" transfers and stickers for the cars "must" be used. And only as indicated on the layout sheet which, ironically in my case, seemed to be missing.

I was being told how to apply them but not where to stick them… but I did already have some ideas of my own.

This was insisted upon because many earlier franchisees had neglected to use many of the stickers (and I can understand why – "Overkill" is the first word that springs to mind, like an over-tattooed footballer, with "Car too small" coming a close second) and those that they had used were used in a haphazard and irregular manner.

There was however, little that they could do to enforce this amongst their current instructors because it was not included in their contracts but, they made clear, from now on, all new instructors, like me, must adhere (sorry again) to the rules (I did refrain from using "*letter* of the agreement" here though!) or risk not receiving any further pupils.

And further, to ensure that the signage was done properly, they insisted upon receiving a photo of my fully-logoed car before they sent me any pupils.

I was taken a little aback by this sudden strictness from a company which, through their ill-fitting suited manager, had projected a relaxed, comfortable and "we are all working together as a team" impression during my signing-on meeting.

But then I remembered the money I was saving and got on with laying out the individual letters on the garage floor as per the very specific instructions.

Now, I don't know if you have ever tried to put stickers on anywhere but, if you have, you will then surely understand my first problem – keeping them in a straight line. I don't remember how many times I nervously applied each letter with gently shaking hands, leant back to get a good perspective, decided it was crooked, removed it and tried again.

Luckily the letters of "NOVICE" and "MORE" were all capitals and, having miraculously managed "MORE" effortlessly, only the "O" of "NOVICE", which was now slightly oval-shaped from all the placing and re-placing, proved a major headache as I had completed the whole thing before I noticed it was slightly "off".

Unfortunately, when I tried to peel it off again I found, because it had been about 10 minutes since I had applied it, it was stuck fast.

I had two options I decided:

1   remove it again with the recommended hair dryer and use it again or

2   leave it and hope that no one noticed.

Sadly I knew I really didn't have the choices that I toyed with above as, even if nobody else noticed my wonky "O", it would, sooner or later, drive me mad and so I would have change it now.

I plugged in the hairdryer.

*"Heat gently from a distance of approximately 10cm on a low heat setting, then simply peel the letter off"* were the clear instructions for removing the transfers.

"Sounds easy," I remember assuring myself.

After several minutes of "gentle and low heat" the offending "O" remained defiantly stuck fast however. With patience now running low, I increased the heat of the hairdryer to more in line with my own rising **temperature**.

This flick of the switch from warm to hot, unfortunately, made little difference to obstructive "O". So, in frustration and feeling the rising irrational yet irresistible anger of "I am going to get this 'O'. It's not going to beat me", I cranked up the medium blow of the by now, glowing hairdryer, to full and, embarrassingly, found myself gritting my teeth and grinning evilly at my – almost – circular target.

Still nothing!

In fact I became hotter and more irate as the unwilted letter yawned widely and roundly back at me.

Then, suddenly, silence…

After 10 minutes at full blast, the exhausted machine in my hand, gasped its last and expired.

"Argghhh!" I yelled from my garage in the otherwise, quiet street and threw the brittle plastic device to the concrete floor before the echo of my anguished outburst had faded.

The "O" remained. Unmoved and, annoyingly, still slightly wonky. But as I glared at it I could see that it was now soft to the touch.

Another idea was born.

I ran to the kitchen, grabbed a wooden spatula and dashed back to the car before all the softening heat had dissipated from the door panel.

I gleefully grinned at the defeated sticker as the wooden tool effortlessly wiped away the obstinate letter from the shiny black door like a fried egg off a Teflon saucepan. "Haha!" I laughed out loud and sat back on my haunches in triumph.

For just a moment I sneered at the wrinkled, shrunken letter that floated feather-like and in pieces to the cold stone floor before I realised that, although the polythene transfer had gone, its glue had left a sticky, grey and stringy "O" shape in its place.

T-Cut, I immediately thought, and set about polishing the rubbery adhesive off.

Eventually, exhausted from my furious buffing, I sat back on the unforgiving and gritty floor and admired my, once again, shiny black door. Having regained my breath and calm, I looked through the jumbled pile of assorted stickers still strewn across the floor for another "O".

Yes, of course, you are already ahead of me.

There was no spare "O" and now I was left with a driver's side door which proudly read "NOVICEnoMORE" and a passenger door reading "N VICEnoMORE" like the announced demise of some obscure Rapper from the late '90s.

My heart sank and I went through my options:

1. Call the office and request more stickers. This, however logical it may seem, may have raised my profile a little higher than I had wanted. Especially at a time when, as I had no intention of using all the stickers, I wanted to keep well below the radar.

2. Leave the door as it was, with one letter missing. The logo was very recognisable in the area anyway so the potential customers would still recognise us, like we all still recognise the Marlboro logo that isn't there on the F1 cars.

3. Improvise!

Now, in spite of my convincing argument for option 2, and in spite of the rationale of option 1, I chose option 3.

Amongst the jigsaw of stickers piled chaotically on the floor, I found a "zero" from one of the larger telephone numbers. It wasn't round (which is ironically why I was in this mess in the first place) and it wasn't quite as big as the other letters (which means I will be worse off!). But it was close.

I set about lining it up properly this time.

With narrow, papery masking tape I created a frame from the letter to sit accurately in (horse, stable-door, bolted, I know). It was like an exercise in geometrical excellence and, with the box of yellow-brown, papery tape around it, the letter looked an even better match for its neighbours than I had imagined.

When, however, I carefully removed the rectangle of tape, the illusion of its size was dispelled and the "zero" posing as an "O", shrank back to its actual size. About 2/3 the size of the "N" and "V" either side of it. It looked just like the "O" in HoVIS.

Now the door read "NoVICEnoMORE" and, in this day of political correctness and CRB checks, promised neither smut nor sleaze to any prospective customer.

Again several options rushed through my mind, including removing the "zero" again, but then I remembered my earlier struggle with the "O" and quickly dismissed this idea. Deciding, more lazily, just to leave it as it was. To quit when I was only slightly behind.

The problem of photos of the car was quickly overcome by photographing just the driver's door, being careful not to include the steering wheel, and then just make a mirror image copy on my laptop. I was careful here too, to crop both photos differently to make them appear as if they were two separate pictures. One showing more front wheel than the other.

Satisfied with my customary bodge of a relatively simple handyman job, and with my photographic deception, I scrunched up the unused letters and transfers and bundled them back into the cardboard tube.

Luckily NnoM were no photographic forensic scientists and my "photo shopping" work was accepted without question. Quite surprisingly as I showed no other stickers on the car!

Anyway, within two days of my emailed fraud, I received my first phone call with client details.

Enthusiastically I grabbed the mobile and proudly introduced myself as a NOVICEnoMORE Instructor for the first time.

However, the friendly, but somewhat disinterested, voice at the other end deflated my excitement a little by pleasantly telling me, as it seems she had a million times before to other ADIs, that she had some new pupils for me.

Wow, I thought, pupils! I might even get a couple in before the end of the week so I listened intently and scribbled furious notes of names, telephone numbers and addresses. I unconsciously heavily underlined the first one's details when, to my surprise, the girl's voice went on to the second pupil and their details. Then, without a pause she gave me a third one and then, unbelievably, a fourth and a fifth!

By number three I had run out of paper and was scrawling over magazines and envelopes. I couldn't believe it! And it was only Monday lunchtime! Five new pupils in one phone call. I didn't get that many in a month a The PAs.

My new best friend at the other end of the phone must have sensed my excitement as she added proudly that they *had* promised at least 30 pupils in the first year and this was designed to get me off to a good start.

I thanked her very much and couldn't wait to get my almost illegible notes into order and to call my new clients.

Those few days at the beginning with NOVICEnoMORE were unbelievable (at first!) and often I noticed that I had a missed call and a voice message from NnoM.

"Uh oh!" I mumbled out loud to myself, "they've made a mistake and given me too many pupils." However when I listened to the message I could not have been more wrong. They had another six, yes six, pupils for me.

My earlier excitement began to ebb away into panic as I tried to get a grip on the situation. I decided to, for the moment, ignore the second wave of pupils and get the first bunch done first.

Calls three and four were less than successful however.

Number three seemed bemused by my call as she already had a NOVICEnoMORE instructor and her test was the following month.

Pupil four didn't answer her phone so I had to leave a message promising to call her again later.

On to pupil five who, in my head, I had initially planned to see on Friday morning as she was in Bar Newton, approximately half way between Weychester and Limeton and therefore a good one hour's drive from Baye where Carol and Colin were at school.

I was actually hoping for more pupils from here as I lived much nearer to Bar Newton than Baye, but beggars can't be choosers and I was happy to get started with one for the time being. But before I could offer her anything else Stacey laid down the rules.

"I can only do Tuesday or Wednesday mornings as I work the other three days."

"How about Saturday?" I quickly replied in an attempt to regain some control.

"No," was her blunt answer and without reason she simply reiterated "Tuesday or Wednesday mornings only."

Already, with just three pupils, I was being forced to either drive large distances between pupils on repeated days or to give up desperately needed clients.

The first five phone calls had secured me just three pupils and, although they hadn't fitted perfectly by any means into my perfect plan, they were still good clients who should at least pay my franchise fee each week.

I then moved onto the next six "leads" on my voicemail. This, I thought, was where I was going to make a profit. (You would, by now, have thought that I would have learned not to count my chickens, but no…)

Of the following six I called, two already had instructors and one had a test booked for the following Friday and just wanted to book a dual-controlled car for the exam.

Another two said they were just enquiring at the moment and were considering other companies still (one hadn't even applied for their provisional licence and the other didn't want lessons until they had passed their, as yet unplanned, theory test).

Finally the sixth "potential client", a neurotic, "mature" sounding lady shrieked panic-stricken down the phone at me that I had no right to call her private mobile number and that she had only filled out the online form to have some information sent to her and hadn't expected to be "harassed, pestered or stalked" by a driver. If anyone was to contact her it would have to be a director.

I gladly agreed never to call her again.

The onslaught of possible pupils continued with a further two calls over the next couple of days delivering details of about 10 more and whilst I was happy that I was receiving contacts at such an early stage, I was a little dismayed at the quality of those leads and the poor conversion rate.

In less than a week I had had 21 possible clients sent my way with only 6 booked for certain.

Then a sickening panic filled my stomach as I remembered the NnoM promise on my contract. A promise that I had heard restated again as the office girl delivered the first five pupils: "at least 30 pupils in the first year."

"I've had 21 pupils already. I hope that they don't stop at 30, otherwise I will have nothing more after next week for the rest of the year."

My fears were far from allayed when I tried to light-heartedly mention it to the office girl when she called again.

Her normally confident and matter-of-fact tone became suddenly nervy and, on three separate occasions – which made me feel that she had done this before – she somehow managed to dodge giving an answer to my clear question and therefore succeeded only in raising my suspicions.

Her final words were delivered in an obviously irritated voice.

"Unfortunately we cannot predict how new pupil numbers will rise or fall throughout the year," she repeated at least twice.

"But," I argued, "some of those you gave me already had instructors and others had no intention of starting lessons."

Her rather hardnosed reply threw a different light on the company that, until now, had made great efforts to portray itself as a friendly, family concern. "We provide you with warm leads but we are not responsible if you are not able to convert them."

# Chapter 6 – All Mapped Out

One of the bonuses of working as a Driving Instructor in such a cosmopolitan town is that I regularly get to meet many different people from many different cultures and backgrounds. All with the same goal however. A small, pink, credit card-sized photo ID allowing them to legally drive.

From their addresses I had already mentally planned who to call first and who would best follow to save driving back and forth unnecessarily.

I called Carol and got a "am I bovvered" girl's voice who seemed to be standing in the middle of a riot at the time. After several attempts to understand her above the background chaos, from which, incidentally, she seemed not to make any attempt to move, I finally gathered that she wanted to start immediately. We agreed a lesson for the following day at twelve o'clock, when she had some free time from school. It didn't quite fit with my imagined timetable but I was sure that I could work around it so I arranged to pick her up from school. "Yeah, okay! Whatever," was her slightly disappointing response.

Phone call two was to what sounded like a young lad who had played truant his whole life from social skills school, although today he appeared to be in the same riot as the previous girl.

I glanced at my watch, 12.30h.

Lunchtime at school, I thought, which explained the chaotic screaming and shrieking around him too. All I could get from him was, "Yeah" or "Nah" and occasionally "Dunno".

In spite of this he did want lessons as soon as possible too and his only free time in the week was 12 'til 2 each lunchtime.

Now, his address was about a mile away from Carol and my plan was to fit one in straight after the other so that I could cover their area once a week and not keep driving back and forth. But, as you have probably already noticed, he has the same time free as Carol and, try as I did to offer later or earlier alternatives, he always had an objection. English lesson, revision class, exam, football training, taking care of his little brother, working at Burger King.

The list went on as my plan disintegrated and I heard Homer Simpson in my mind. "Doh!"

I booked him for twelve o'clock the day after Carol. The final insult came when he confirmed that pick-up would be at the same school as her.

Carol, a bright and lively girl, fell squarely into the "random chaotic" category with no fear of asking a question.

I taught her from a week after her 17th birthday, when her mother had surprised her with a gift of lessons, and she had made rapid progress through the syllabus and light work of the manoeuvres.

Her only enemy was her concentration. Or rather her lack of it. Once she had mastered each skill, she did it almost without thinking, and this is where her mind drifted through a wide range of, apparently, unconnected subjects.

One Friday evening whilst attempting to work our way safely onto a very busy and congested roundabout, looking for a brief gap in the seemingly constant stream of buses, trucks and cars, Carol asked, "Do you like my jumper? My mum reckons it's too small and the arms are too long."

I was amused by her chaotic thought pattern but nevertheless impressed by her calm in a situation which would, and had, turned several of my other pupils to jelly. I don't think she really expected or required a reply as she coolly negotiated her way onto, and off of, the car-carousel, but merely blurted out a recycled fragment of conversation from earlier in the day.

This, however, was not her only mind-wandering moment. In the weeks that followed I was treated to, "My friend Gale is really gay," whilst sitting at traffic lights longing for a green.

No further explanation was given as to why Gale had been subjected to such an accusation and as to whether she was "*really* gay" or just "really *gay*". Only poor Gale knows.

Another totally isolated gem whilst reversing around a corner was, "My dad went to the dentist today." For what reason, I don't know I don't think she did either so I left it there.

Carol did, however, now and again ask the odd question to which she really did want a reply. Whilst pulled over at the side of the road discussing her driving, the inevitable subject of "The Test" arose and the, so-called, "show me, tell me" questions that she may be asked at the beginning of the examination. Luckily, I thought, I had a copy of the questions and began asking her a few to re-assure her that they were mainly straight forward.

"1 Show me how you would check that the direction indicators work on this car?

2 Tell me how you would check the parking brake for excessive wear?"

I went on, oblivious to what must have been a cloud of disinterest which had descended upon Carol.

"3 Open the bonnet and show me how you would check the oil level."

"Where's your cervix?" Carol interrupted.

Now, I *can* see a sort of line of thought here but was nevertheless stunned by the bluntness of the question from a 17-year-old girl until I saw her nonchalant and unflinching face and realised her question was genuine.

"I overheard my sister talking about hers to my mum last night, but didn't get what she meant."

"Ask your mum," I suggested, half amused by the shock of the question but also pleased to have glimpsed the embers of innocence of a child otherwise lost to the smart answering and lippy teenager projected to the world.

When it came to confident, lippy teenagers, Colin was a modern-day character from *Oliver Twist*. Quite short but wiry, his mop of unkempt blond hair was always wedged under a white baseball cap. Its peak, tilted skyward like a Jemima Puddleduck bonnet, scuffed the cloth car ceiling above his driving seat each time he checked his mirrors. In spite of this irritation Colin refused to remove it and I began to wonder what he had to hide. Did he have a monk's bald patch? Did he have two small red horns under there?

But for such a short, even delicate appearance Colin portrayed anything but fragility. From his deep, older than his years, voice (half fashionably "cor-blimey" gangster, half Dorset yokel) to his weathered and leathery furrowed face – more suited to a farm worker in his 50s than to a 17 year old – Colin's aura screamed rogue and, more immediately concerning, BOY RACER!

Each time I picked him up from his parents' five-bedroom, detached new-build home surrounded by neatly trimmed privet and lawns but suffocated by the obligatory array of two Nissan 4x4s, a square, featureless, white, washing machine-esque caravan and a 20ft yacht hull, Colin had invariably forgotten his lesson and appeared at the door, bleary-eyed from his pit, dressed only in a pair of shorts but, yes you've guessed it, with his cap on.

After a brief rushing around behind the ajar door, he would re-appear – cake, biscuit or bread in hand and ready for the surprise of a lesson. No matter how many times this happened and no matter how many times I reminded him at the end of the previous unexpected lesson, Colin never got to grips with the schedule.

Despite however, all this time management chaos, Colin was a quick learner and was soon relaxed behind the wheel, confidently negotiating any obstacle or hazard thrown his way.

Consequently our routes took us to ever further points from his local patch and into neighbouring towns and villages and it seemed that he had a story for every area we passed.

"Down there. That lane there. That's where I come off me 'ped." He snorted. "Me mates pissed 'emselves coz I ripped me jeans an' I 'ad to ride 'ome wiv me arse 'anging out." His smiling, smoke-cracked, bass voice shook the car.

Passing one of the many quaint Whimburton pubs, Colin suddenly pointed to an old Transit van slumped in the corner of the car park. "That's me band's van," he boasted, and for a moment I was impressed until he repainted the scene with the brush of open honesty. "It's a knackered heap of crap. We done a gig there last week an' the bastard wouldn't go afterwards so we dumped it.

Don't think they've sussed it yet that we ain't coming back."

When I pointed out that they'll trace it back to him via the registration number he told me they'd already thought of that and removed the number plates.

"We ain't that thick you know," he laughed, but then his face dropped with perfect comic timing, "But we 'ad to walk 'ome wiv our guitars an' gear. It's about five miles. An' it was pissing dahn."

Each lesson brought another gem which either made me laugh out loud or squirm at his words and what they revealed.

"Wow, look. Look!" he suddenly barked as we circled the same short route for the fourth time to practise a particularly difficult roundabout. "It's a war car be'ind us. Yeah, it's a German war car."

Alarmed at his Houdini-like attempts to contort in his driving seat to get a better look at the fascinating vehicle, I shrieked at him to watch the road ahead whilst I looked in my mirror to see the reason for his excitement.

Immediately following us was a rectangular, German army grey, VW beach buggy-style jeep. I laughed and I told him that it was probably a VW Beetle chassis and air-cooled engine with a light "Mini-Moke"-like body. I had tried to sound as if I knew what I was talking about and it seemed to work as Colin fell silent.

Encouraged by this I went further. "It's got an original P plate so it's from about 1975 or 6."

His eyes re-lit. "Well that's about right then for the war innit?"

But what Colin lacked in general knowledge he more than made up for with pure cheek and bravado.

An uneventful lesson was approaching the halfway mark and thus we were about the furthest point away from his home when, after successfully guiding us around an extremely sharp bend, Colin announced, "The other night I saw the police make a right balls-up of that corner."

I smiled but, without showing too much interest, I asked, "What were you doing watching police cars right out here?"

"Nah I wasn't watchin' 'em. I got arrested." He grinned proudly.

"What?" My interest swelled.

"Yeah, they thought they saw me on CCTV nicking stuff, so they nicked me at 'ome an' brought me to the police station here."

He went on, "Funny fing was that they showed me the video and *I* thought it was me too! I was only that I didn't remember being there otherwise I would have thought I did it."

I laughed but could think of no words to continue with.

Colin assisted. "I was in the back of their van when he took the corner too tight an' hit the kerb. I really got froan arand a bit."

"Did you tell him how to do it properly?" I weakly asked, not wanting to show any encouragement but nevertheless interested in the story and half expecting him to say "*yes*".

I was disappointed, but still amused, by his, "Nah, I was bricking it!"

Annifrid, like her Abba namesake, was tall, pale and flame-haired but came from St Petersburg in Russia rather than Norway. She was generally a rather cool, expressionless character but friendly nonetheless, occasionally allowing herself a brief, sigh-like laugh as her tenseness momentarily slumped to relax before re-gathering her rigid body language.

Her mystery was enhanced by her vagueness about herself. She always avoided the general questions of where she worked, only imprecisely hinting that she worked "only at night" and "in a hotel usually" and I always had to meet her on the street, never at an address. Her manner, however, was entirely different and ultimately stood in the way of her quest (for that was what it was to become) to obtain a licence.

Whenever I pointed out her minor faults – faults which were later to return to haunt her when taking her many tests – her attitude was to shrug and roll out, "Ah vell, it is not such a big problem" in a heavy, rounded Russian accent.

No matter how many times I assured her and tried to impress upon her it *was* important and could become a "big problem", I never managed to shake her from her laid-back state.

On the other hand, adding to the conundrum of her personality, if *she* perceived a problem to be major, she was merciless with her own self-criticism.

A typical example of this would surface at least once a lesson when she would lift the clutch pedal a little too quickly when changing down through the gears, causing a brief but noticeable jerk as the car re-adjusted to the new, considerably lower, speed. This is a very common fault amongst inexperienced (and quite often also experienced!) drivers, but with time and practice this usually disappears.

But to Annifrid this was the most serious fault in her driving and its every appearance was greeted with an exasperated roll of her eyes to the sky and an angry grunting rush of air through her teeth, like a serving tennis player.

The fact that she regularly crossed the centre line of the road she was reversing into during her manoeuvres when backing around a corner or that, when trying to execute what was previously called a three point turn, she always hit the kerbs, was routinely shrugged off with the generally resigned (and somewhat amusing), "I always have problems with my manures."

Poor girl.

Annifrid had just failed her 8th test when I saw her last.

Not because she couldn't drive and certainly not because she was nervous or unsure of herself, but purely because her attitude remained unshaken and her approach to the whole task unaltered from her first lesson.

"Why such a big deal about the mirrors all the time?" she asked me after her 5th test.

She will probably always remain an enigma, but I know what image I was conjuring up of this hotel, night-working girl who insisted on being picked up on a street corner. Each new detail probably adding up to a wildly inaccurate conclusion, but then again maybe she tapped into my train of thought and enjoyed positively encouraging me in my confusion.

Even after her last test she added to the mystery as her mobile number was suddenly and immediately unobtainable and she never re-appeared again.

Other pupils can be the complete opposite.

When I first saw Lee stroll cockily across the road to me for his first lesson I knew exactly what I was getting.

White, Reebok tracksuit bottoms, white (but slightly greyer) Adidas tracksuit jacket and a white F&F baseball cap with sky-blue side panels, peak curled down at either end to form a smooth arch across his forehead. On his feet he wore grimy, scuffed, but of course, white trainers starkly contrasting with his black socks.

Yes, Lee was a chav.

But contrary to their collective image, Lee was a happy and friendly chap/chav. He was very open and happy to discuss his work as a bricklayer's apprentice. He was proud that he had worked on some "top celeb" that I had never heard of's house in on the beach, "proppa lush" was how he described it, and he also told me that he had had a car when he was 15 and had been driving it around.

"In a field behind me 'ouse," he rapidly suffixed and grinned with guilty pride as my face betrayed my amazement that, firstly he had been driving so young and secondly, he had freely volunteered the information to me, a total stranger not more than 10 minutes ago! He continued to smile as he went on to add that his dad had sold the car just days before his 17th birthday.

Again my face pre-empted my comment and Lee read it. "Coz it was fallin' apart," he grinned widely again. "But some mug bought it."

I suddenly didn't want to like him but his simple honesty with regard to his dishonesty and an innocent lack of guilt made me reluctantly concede and we got along quite well.

Lee was one of my first few pupils after moving to The South Coast and the way he spoke scared me. Not because of the words or any strong language he used (although he did pad out his, sometimes lacking, vocabulary with the blasé use of "Fs" and worse) but because of his heavy Dorset / West Country twang, coupled with his pseudo-Caribbean-hoody parlance. Delivered at the speed of light, I grasped about as much as I would have, had he been speaking Klingon with a Geordie accent:

"Gottagetroundaolegitinnit."

*"I have got to get around the old man, haven't I"* was a reference to getting past an elderly cyclist during an overtaking lesson. This took two or three translation requests from me and some exasperated pointing at the wobbly old boy in front of us by Lee before I got the gist.

Further repetition was necessary for:

"wegonnachillinaminitcozeyesgaspiny'no!" followed by a simplified version delivered by Lee slowly and deliberately at a higher volume for the dumbfounded imbecile sat beside him. "FAG - BREAK?"

His concentration noticeably dipped during each lesson and the cigarette stop became a regular feature for him after about an hour of his two-hour lesson.

He would literally jump out of the barely stationary car to pull out a faded plastic pouch of loose tobacco and Rizla papers to roll a cigarette so frantically that most of the tobacco he had just piled onto the open paper dropped silently out of each end of the roll-up and back into his stash. This ritual roll-up took much longer than the actual smoking of the nearly empty fag-paper which burned almost as fast as a cartoon gunpowder fuse to the barrel. One draw and the flame was at his lips.

That done, Lee was back with me, in body and mind, for the remainder of the lesson and firing rapid streams of accent distorted words for me to disentangle.

One favourite request was: "youfinkeyesreddyfordajulies?" which stumped me upon its first appearance.

Lee, again, had to help. "The julies?" his voice questioned.

I still looked blank and apologetic.

"The Ju- Lies," he repeated at a still slower pace.

Still nothing registered and the car fell silent at my embarrassment.

"Y'kno. Somerset Highway. The fast one," he tried in desperation.

Jackpot. I got it!

My whole body relaxed as I triumphantly confirmed it with him. "Oh, the dual carriageway. The Dualies."

However, in spite of his mandatory cigarette sometimes he still seemed tired or distracted, or both.

On one occasion our progress had been slow throughout the lesson, so I decided to cut out some of the new work I was planning to introduce and to concentrate upon consolidating Lee's confidence in everyday situations. It seemed as if his learning curve had plateaued a little over the last couple of lessons and I wanted him to get his "feeling" back for the situations like junctions and roundabouts.

However, the more we practised – then stopped to discuss what went well or not so well – the more his concentration faded and the worse his driving became. So we decided to head home a few minutes early.

We were approaching Lee's road from the main high street with the junction being about 100 metres away on our left and, having driven it many times before with him I let my own concentration lapse and relaxed a bit.

"Turn left…" I almost routinely began, assuming Lee knew the way home. (Never assume, I hear you all say. It will make an ASS out of U and ME, and on this occasion it really did.)

Before I could continue the sentence Lee swung us, in fourth gear and at 30 mph, into the one-car wide, school entrance immediately to our left and just before his home junction.

When we finally hit the rock solid "stall wall" just inside the school gates and thanked our lucky stars that no one was coming out at the time, my open-mouthed silence was enough to prompt the similarly shocked teenager beside me to justify his madness.

"Well, *you*toldmetodoit,anat."

In the stunned stillness of the stranded, red-lit dashboard, I could only hear Quentin's (Danielle's) patronizing voice telling me that he told me so. Unfortunately though, there was no "out of role" option to save the situation.

## Chapter 7 – From D.I.C.K.S. to Testees

At last the big day had arrived for Richard. After months of kerbing and scuffing the wheels and looking in the left mirror then signalling right, he had finally managed more coordination in his driving than he seemed to have whilst walking and his test was here.

What Richard didn't know was that although this was his first test, this was also *my* first test as an instructor so I was as nervous as him having been told by The D.I.C.K.S. that if you had a poor pass rate, customers would look it up and never use me.

When confronted by my pupils and their parents as to my pass rate and how long I had worked as an instructor, my stock answer in those early days was, "Oh, quite a while down here and before that I was in South West London." Vague enough for it not to be untrue but not really answering their question I know!

A confident boy, Richard moaned, very teenager-like, that the "old-git" of an examiner on his friend's first test had had it in for him. "He didn't want to pass him from the moment they met," he complained, but his ramblings of a conspiracy against today's youth was, I was told by other instructors, the usual response of shaky drivers looking to shift the blame.

Nevertheless, having seen his friend's fairly proficient driving when picking up Richard, I was inclined to feel that, although he had maybe exaggerated it a bit, Richard's mate had been a victim of, at least, an obstructive examiner.

The first thing I noticed was his uncharacteristically serious face as we walked to the car. "You okay?" I smiled to lighten the mood.

"Yeah," was his slightly sarcastically tinged reply. "Bet I'm gonna get that old bloke," he continued, revealing his anxiety.

Try as I might, all the assurances I could muster, including that there were so many examiners that the odds against getting him were stacked in Richard's favour, failed to change his mood or more accurately, lift his fear.

Our drive to the test centre was unusually quiet and I could see his nerves in his driving as we approached – and bumped across the kerb into – the otherwise anonymous road.

"You *know* you can do it," I rather limply encouraged again. "You have consistently shown me how well you can drive so now it's just another 40 minutes."

His lack of response told me I wasn't winning but I still had one last attempt. "Just trust yourself and your judgement. It's usually right. You know that."

"Of course I know I'm good enough," Richard finally snapped, "but it doesn't matter how good I am coz that skinny old git will find fault somewhere."

"Oh, I'm sure that's not the case," I tried to insist but even I could hear my lack of conviction, "they are all professionals. They will deal with each case with an open mind. If you are good enough on the day, you will pass."

"You *are* joking?" he retorted, shaking his head and strode off toward the test centre entrance.

Now, when I say "test centre" you may imagine a modern, sleek, grey and glass, purpose-built office unit offering a comfortably light and warm waiting room for the, understandably nervous, candidates whilst they await their examiners. Well, you couldn't be more wrong.

Just approaching the front door you got an accurate sense of the place. It is, unmistakeably, an old shop surrounded by many other vacant old shops outside which you could imagine large groups of hooded youth congregate at night to plan their latest claim on achieving an ASBO or compare their false Caribbean accents.

From outside it was difficult to see inside through the peeling, stick-on tint on the bottom half of the windows. However, above this dark, opaque visual barrier could be seen the vertical hanging blinds. Originally white, they now hung lifeless and jaundiced from years of obvious neglect and fingering from curious instructors watching their pupils depart on the tests.

Above the glass and wood grocery store door is what one assumes was the reaction of a previously "unsuccessful" candidate (They don't say "failed" any more!).

A large splash of white paint from what appears not to have been a paint-ball, rather a paint-football and from whose impact point had run several skinny, white snakes of liquid vertically downwards stopping just above the doorframe to form a giant albino squid.

Once inside, the inexplicably hushed atmosphere seemed to immediately intimidate everyone into a whisper and put pressure upon bladders. "You know where the loo is?" are always the first words uttered upon crossing the threshold.

Richard was no exception and immediately disappeared to the small room only to return looking paler than before. This, I assumed, was to do with his heightened nervous state and nothing to do with the previous occupant of the cubicle.

Whilst away I had chosen seats for us having surveyed the regular, low, dark-blue square, cushioned chairs and picked the least stained pair. Maybe the queue for the loo was sometimes too long for some people, I immediately thought, then dismissed it as too awful to contemplate and reassured myself that the patches on the seat covers matched those on the carpet-tiled floor and thus must be tea and coffee stains. Holding onto that belief, and my breath, I sat delicately down.

In the meantime Richard had returned and sat beside me in silence and we were soon joined by several middle-aged men and women instructors with their teenaged pupils in various crimes against fashion, both slightly embarrassed by each other.

Several smiley plump girls, wearing clothes designed for size zero models and nose-rings, accepted the directions to the toilet and disappeared into the dark corridor to be followed by one or two under-fed boys with strange, but apparently fashionable swept forward hairstyles and jeans belted way below their backsides showing market-bought fake Calvin Kleins, slunk coolly off for a wee only to be flustered when they found the toilet occupied and they faced returning, unrelieved, to their seat or lurking perv-like outside the flimsy door and bear aural witness to the events inside.

At that moment we were rescued from our pre-occupation with the bathroom shifts as the "Do Not Enter" office door began to open to reveal a pack of Hi-Vis vested and clipboard-grasping examiners huddling through the narrow doorway.

The hushed room fell silent as the shaking pupils strained to hear their names.

One by one the room emptied of youth until, ominously, only Richard remained and I felt a tangible wave of relief from the other instructors as they allowed themselves to smile sympathetically in our direction.

The door then opened again and the inevitable was confirmed.

"It's him!" Richard hissed from the corner of his mouth as the gaunt, grey-haired and cowboy-hattedflat-capped man before us artificially sang out Richard's full name in a "I've done this a thousand times before but have been told that I must make it sound more genuine" way.

Similarly he rattled, stream of consciousness-like, through the required, "Please read the statement and sign in your usual signature if you agree and you have lived at the address on your licence for at least 6 of the last 12 months." Somewhat like a policeman reading you your rights as he arrests you, it has to be done but he really can't be bothered to inject any interest into it.

Richard, having signed, was instantly reduced from cocky teenager to a small boy being led off to the Head Master's office, turned to me and meekly asked, "Will you come with me please?"

Now, you have to remember this was before examiners were obliged to ask if the candidate would like someone to accompany them, so as I nodded my agreement, the examiner's face blackened.

"You ask *me*, whether I will allow him to come along," he growled in front of the other waiting instructors. "I'm in charge of this situation, not him." He threw a disgusted glance at me.

"Okay," Richard shakily continued, "sorry, but can my instructor come with me, please?"

"If he must," was the dismissive reply. "Now lead the way out to your car," he mumbled impatiently further.

Richard apparently heard only the first half of the reply because he politely stood back and held the door open for the examiner.

"What did I tell you, boy?" the poisonous hollow, grey face spat. "We are not going to get on well if you don't listen to me."

You've already decided that you're not going to get along, I thought to myself as I attempted to follow both of them through the old shop door which the examiner allowed to swing shut in my face. Stunned by his ignorance I glanced back at the similarly shocked witnesses in the waiting room for some kind of support.

"Good luck, mate!" one sympathised, "Faylum's on form today."

"I'd book another test now if I were you," another encouragingly added.

Richard's mate hadn't been exaggerating.

Once in the car our tormentor for the next 40 minutes or so immediately began his mumbled monologue in an artificially undulating voice of what to expect and what he expected of Richard. He managed this apparent "must" without once looking up from his clipboard until, having fastened his seatbelt, he threw an unblinking stare at Richard and instructed with a question, almost daring Richard to object, "I shall be calling you Richard throughout the test?"

The shaking boy nodded silently.

"Okay Richard, I've explained how things are going to work on this test so let's get on with it," he continued his impatience and then to my surprise he turned to me seated in the back.

"And you," his grey, thin and angular face hissed at me, "you know the score don't you? Not a peep from you or he fails. Got it?" and swung his poisonous glare back to the battered black clipboard.

Shell-shocked at the onslaught of the last few minutes, I did as ordered and so was surprised when Richard apologetically and shakily piped up to ask, "Sorry, but I didn't catch your name?"

I cheered inside. Well done, I thought, give him some back.

But my joy was short-lived when our, as yet, anonymous host replied with a well-rehearsed, "I didn't tell you. If you want to know, look at the name badge."

Now, being as the said name badge was on the left breast pocket of his shirt, beneath his open Hi-Vis vest, Richard had no chance of seeing it without getting out of the car, walking around to the passenger side and reading it before returning to his driver's seat. Given the crushing blow that his mini fight-back had just suffered, this was extremely unlikely.

I, on the other hand, had already sneaked a glimpse of the badge as we had walked to the car.

Victor Faylum, I sniggered to myself nervously. Really?

In spite of the obvious ordeal for Richard, the 40 minutes seemed to fly by for me and Mr Faylum sighed the words, "Pull over on the left-hand side, somewhere safe, legal and convenient and switch off the engine."

Bumping the kerb as he obeyed, Faylum tutted and shook his head at Richard's incompetence but seemed to lighten his mood when he was able to deliver his verdict.

"The test is now over and, of course, you have failed."

(I thought they weren't supposed to say that anymore!)

His eyes lit up further without his thin, tight lips curling to a smile as he asked, script perfect, "Would you like me to point out and explain your faults?" but continued nevertheless without waiting for a reply, rattling off the three main faults that he had failed Richard with.

I got the distinct impression that Victor Faylum quite enjoyed this part of the test although neither Richard nor me were truly listening properly.

"Quite honestly," he continued to put the boot in, "there were so many mistakes I wouldn't have time to list them all now, but here's a fail sheet." (I didn't think they were supposed to say that anymore?)

He seemed to like the "F" word. "It lists them all."

Then, with the most insincere farewell I have ever heard he sprung from the car like a spring from a watch with "Goodbye, have a nice day and take care."

"Er, Mr Faylum?" I attempted to ask a question as he strode away but was silenced by the darkness that instantly returned to his face at my insolence at using his name and his slow deliberate words accompanied by a single, arthritic index finger aimed at me.

"Ah-ah! Not a peep I said!"

My initiation into this enclave of 1970's style customer service left me stunned and made it very difficult to put future pupils at ease by convincingly dismissing the rumours of psychological torture or just plain rudeness.

Victor Faylum's name is even frequently mentioned on several social networking sites as the one to avoid.

The one who will definitely fail you and they even credit him with single-handedly holding down the test centre's pass rate below 45% compared with other nearby centres who consistently achieve a more typical 55% plus. A bit too flattering I think for someone who really just appears to hate his job and toys with his victims in order to inject some enjoyment into it. According to the rumour mill, he even enjoys the infamy and, fully aware of his notoriety, plays to the gallery in order to build his dubious, villainous reputation.

Now, you might think that such a display of prehistoric customer service would be easily remedied nowadays with a written complaint to Mr F's superior. But therein lay the problem. The general consensus of opinion amongst the cruelly, but accurately named "failures" was that if they complained about their treatment, that their "cards would be marked" for all future tests and they would be earmarked for tests with Faylum for all eternity. Or at least all the examiners would close ranks and none of them would ever pass the poor teenaged wretches.

This impression was further compounded by several anonymous (presumably for fear of further examination persecution and not just through embarrassment at having failed a few tests, surely?) online contributors who thought they'd be clever and switch their test from Weychester to the next nearest test centre at Banmouth, only to again be confronted by the flat-capped Faylum.

It's, I would always tell my students, quite common that examiners help out in neighbouring centres from time to time but, as with stories of the Bermuda Triangle and UFOs, once a rumour was floated it was quickly further inflated by more, often dubious, "evidence" and thereafter proved extremely difficult to sink. Conspiracy always being more appealing than the dull facts.

When, however, a pupil was sufficiently incensed or angered by their test experience and they did put together a letter of complaint, the process, as I discovered, was laborious.

Firstly, if they wrote to the Senior Examiner at Weychester – i.e. Mr F's boss, they received no reply.

When the pupil in question was with me, I called on their behalf to enquire as to: 1, whether the letter was received and, 2, when they could expect a reply?

I was astounded by the response of the hitherto reasonable and friendly SE. He told me that they had no means of writing letters or emails from the Weychester office! So effectively the complaint was ignored at the local level.

My pupil was told that they should write again and this time to address it to the DSA head office. But only if they "really felt it necessary."

This done, the only reaction of the DSA was to send an observer to sit in on a few tests with Faylum.

Of course, on his best behaviour, Mr Faylum passed this test with flying colours but afterwards had the cheek to claim victimisation by his employers and reported the incident to his union.

No further observations were made.

David was my latest project. Just 17, he was itching (quite literally sometimes) to get driving.

We started our lessons in mid-November but, nevertheless David, a typical surfer boy (i.e. long, blond, curly hair, sea-bleached fingernails and even a "Hey dude!" language of his own) without fail, bounded, Labrador-like from his front door in three-quarter length, cut-down jeans and flip-flops.

Despite his inappropriate attire, David was a quick, albeit nervous, learner and made rapid progress. From his first moments behind the steering wheel his posture betrayed his edginess.

Although not particularly tall, David seemed to believe he was about a foot shorter than he actually was and always slid the driver's seat fully forward and pumped it up to its highest level.

The eventual effect was to make it appear that David was hugging the wheel to find some kind of security or comfort from the obvious terror he associated with driving... Or perhaps me!

Try as I might during those early lessons to tell him of the dangers of sitting unnecessarily close to the wheel, and thus the airbag, David refused to relinquish his embrace. This grip led to other problems such as him having to sit on the front edge of his seat to maintain the hold which, in turn, led to his knees bumping the steering column when he pressed or lifted the clutch.

This most uncomfortable looking "comfort" for David lasted for most of our first five or six hours of tuition until he finally clicked as to why he went home totally exhausted after every lesson. The physical effort of continuously tensing all your body's muscles for two hours would be enough to send me to my bed for the rest of the week.

The enlightenment led to a slight, but only slight, slump in his rigid driving posture, a gentle loosening of his white-knuckled grip on the steering wheel and his ability to move his head and neck two or three degrees either side to look into his mirrors occasionally.

I mentioned David's itching earlier. Initially I wondered what kind of wildlife he was introducing to my car each Saturday morning until I realised from his, sometimes, frantic clawing at his scalp and rapid boring and agitation of his ears with his little fingers, that he had already been for an early morning surf. Hence his ears were still carrying samples of Dorset's coastal waters and his drying hair was depositing irritating sea-salt on his well-forested head. At least I hope that was what it was. I never actually asked outright and the alternatives were too gross to consider.

But these characteristics were not David's only burdens in life. Somehow – and thinking back to our first meeting along with his parents at their front door – this was clear then too.

David, or rather his eyes, had the unhappy knack of attracting any passing foreign object into them. Dust, pollen, leaves, insects, seatbelts, twigs, crisps to name but a few, all ended up in one or other of his eyes at some point.

At the aforementioned first meeting I greeted his mum and dad but David hung back in the shadows of their front door, bent slightly forward, repeatedly drawing deep, sharp breaths through his clenched teeth, mumbling "ahhs" and "oohs" to himself whilst furiously rubbing at his left eye with a loosely balled fist.

I could almost have been guaranteed that during each lesson David would, at one point or another, have to stop the car and sort out his vision.

The cries, "Ow! My Eye!" or "Help, help, help! Can't see," at first scared the living daylights out of me as I feared he'd suffered a serious injury or seizure, but eventually became synonymous with David, Saturday mornings and scratching.

An attack could spring from any quarter at any time during our two hours in the car and therefore I learned that I had to be constantly on my guard to grab immediately the steering wheel that he would instantly release in order to frantically rub at his injury.

On one occasion I turned on the air conditioning to clear the steamed-up window and dust blew from the vent directly into his left eye.

"Yeeow! It's in my eye," he howled from behind the two bony-fingered hands now covering his entire face whilst we continued to freewheel along the busy high street.

Another time we had managed to complete the lesson without an eye incident or "Eye-cident" as we came to know them.

I delivered a complimentary debrief after a successful drive but as he unbuckled the seatbelt he felt an irresistible urge to scratch through his blond locks and, in doing so, flicked the shiny steel tongue of the belt over his right shoulder and slapping him in the eye on the way.

"Ahhh! Ahhh! Ow, ow, ow. Can't see again. My eye!" he yelled blindly as he stumbled from and around the car and disappeared into his parents' front garden.

Sporting the yellowish green tinge of a mini-black eye, David again arrived enthusiastically for his lesson and we joked about his seatbelt assault and hoped that it was an "eye-solated" incident.

He groaned and shook his head at my "dad" humour and off we drove.

However, is spite of his liability to eye injury, David made great progress with his driving and thus, only a few short weeks after Richard, David was up for his test too.

It was an overcast morning with a frown-inducing whitish light to the day when a David I had not seen before emerged from his front door. He was wearing full-length jeans, a Fred Perry style T-shirt, socks and trainers. His hair was neatly combed back from his forehead and he tightly grasped his licence and theory test paper.

"Wow!" I commented, open-mouthed. "I nearly didn't recognise you."

"Shup Dude," he nervously laughed, "Don't want anything to go wrong." He continued, "Look," he tapped his upper chest where sunglasses hung from the three open buttons of his shirt. "Nothin's gonna get in my eye today coz I heard from my mates that there's like some old geezer at the test place that's a real bugger."

I laughed nervously and dismissively but it didn't work.

David went on, "He's got a serious bad rep apparently. Loads of real funny names for him online." He grinned but soon came back to scared. "A fly in the eye is last thing I need if I get him."

"Who's that then?" I attempted to feign a nonchalant ignorance to dodge the inevitable questions.

"Everyone knows him," David opened up and looked at me with disbelief at my denial, "and everyone's got a horror story about him. Seems like he hasn't passed anyone for four years."

He over-inflated the story to prod me for a reaction and I tried to gently dismiss his obvious fears with carefully chosen words of re-assurance. That all examiners were highly professional, that they would *never* (an ulcer immediately sprung up on my tongue!) be unfair or biased. I even found myself using Mr F's own unofficial, but frankly implausible, propaganda that the "older" examiners had the highest pass rate at the test centre.

My arguments, however, were unconvincing, even to my own ears and seemed to be focussing the attention further upon the examiner rather than the test so I casually wound up the chat with, "Well anyway, there are about 15 examiners so it's very unlikely that you'll get him anyway."

Yes, you guessed it. He got him!

"David Smith," mumbled a thin, almost exasperated voice from the back of the fruit bowl room of yellow and orange Hi-Vis vests on rounded middle-aged men that successfully absorbed any sound.

"David Smith," he repeated with no attempt to raise his voice above the citrus crowd before him. Sensing that David had still not heard, (sea water maybe?) I nudged him and pointed him in Faylum's direction.

David sprung to attention like a surprised cat and thrust his right hand forward in greeting to his examiner as he had seen the other pupils do with their testers.

Mr F, however, stopped short and, in front of a full room, looked distastefully at David's hand then completely ignored it. "Don't you know your own name?" he hissed in a reference to having to repeat his hushed call. "Not a very good start. Where's your licence?"

Embarrassed by the humiliation, David's face reddened as he dropped his hand and the full room fell silent.

Faylum then went on with his blurred blurb regarding David's address and insurance on the car before he, "Major Vic" – one of the names David had picked up online for his examiner in a clear reference to his weakness for giving major faults to candidates as soon and as often as possible– nodded to the door and ordered, "Lead the way."

David had the face of a condemned man on the long walk to the gallows but managed just a faint, hopeless smile as he left the room.

"STOP." We all jumped in the waiting room at Faylum's order to David just outside the, by now, closed door.

"STOP!" he repeated immediately. His irritation was already clear.

"Sorry!" David unnecessarily apologised, "I'm a bit nervous."

He received no reply but Faylum continued, "Read that number plate," and pointed to a distant car.

"Ow!" David replied, "Sorry, got something in my eye."

The irritated examiner threw David a withering look and added, "Stop stalling or I have to stop the test right now."

"But…" David didn't continue, seeing the futility but rubbed wildly at his, by now, bloodshot eye and tried again.

Having eventually, fluently read out the registration, David had obviously disappointed his companion who then waved him forward.

"Lead me to your car," his mumble reinstated, the pair slowly ambled away from the test centre doorway and their disbelieving audience breathed again as David was again heard to apologise and concede again that, "I am a bit nervous."

To which Faylum stopped his walk and snapped, "I know that, you already told me once." Then pointing his finger directly at David went on, "Nerves have nothing to do with it. Either you can drive or you can't. Which is it?"

David did not reply but, open-mouthed, slowly put on his sunglasses whilst he continued his forlorn traipse to the waiting car.

Mr F reignited his stride to almost a goosestep and followed.

"Sorry, but I'm glad *you* got him and not me." One of my fellow instructors broke the silence.

As usual my feeling of helplessness soon dissolved into resignation as I watched each pupil walk nervously to their cars, forget how to unlock them with the remote control and set off the alarm with the key in the lock. This prefixed their wiping the windscreen as they set off instead of signalling and finally bunny-hopping the suffering vehicle to the end of the narrow side street and disappearing from view.

It was out of my hands now.

However, on each occasion I went back over all the points in my mind, that we had covered during their lessons to be sure that I had missed nothing. A bit late I know, but it was a reflex ritual I could not stop.

For me, the 30-odd minutes (Faylum was always last out, first back, just about covering the 33 minimum requirement) of his test flew by. David's return was a much smoother affair than his departure although he did park some 200 metres from the test centre entrance and far enough from the kerb for his examiner to be justified in ordering a taxi to the pavement.

I began my brisk, half excited, half dreading march to hear the, so-called, debrief of David's test. More accurately described by many as the verdict or even sentencing.

As I approached the lonely, almost abandoned-looking car from the front, I could clearly see both David and his tormentor. My heart sank along with my step rate. It was like watching a silent Punch and Judy show, with Mr F waving his right index finger closely at David's face, then pointing front and back before gesticulating animatedly with his tattered clipboard.

David (or Judy) on the other hand, gawped, open-mouthed at his verbal assailant and visibly flinched each time the evil pantomime baddie in the seat beside him flailed another accusing finger.

The onslaught continued as I reached the car and, although they had both seen me approach, neither looked up or acknowledged my spare part presence beside the passenger door, awaiting my invitation to listen to the "constructive criticism" from the qualified driving professional. That invitation never came and I stooped idly outside for another 2 or 3 minutes trying to decipher the deep, muffled tones from within, like listening to a row through the wall in the next door flat.

The one-way conversation stopped abruptly with Faylum swinging the door open and himself into the gutter before reaching the pavement. "And I didn't even mention your parking." He crouched and barked back into the car before finally turning to me and sneering, "You took your time. You missed the debrief."

I swallowed my anger but glared at the thin, grey-faced and poisonous git (I guess I didn't swallow it too well after all!) as he almost goose-stepped back to the test centre.

From my position on the kerb I bent forward to catch David's eye through the still open door. "That went well then," were his only words as he vigorously rubbed his right eye behind his sunglasses.

Was he crying? Or, in spite of the precautions, had something still managed to invade his optical space?

Julia Jimenez was a real character. Only about 5' 4" tall, her thick, almost black, shoulder-length hair and dark eyes told you, before she spoke, of her Latin roots. When she did speak her gentle, yet strong Spanish lisped voice was an aural delight.

Being in her early twenties she had already driven before as a learner, but in Argentina, so from the word go with me, she handled the car well but just needed to catch up with the rules and regulations over here to get her British licence.

Her usually excellent English however, occasionally let her down but she confidently improvised.

Whilst pulling away on an uphill slope she stalled the engine. Irritated with herself she immediately let me know that she knew what she had done wrong. "I know, I know." She shook her head at the simple error. "Not enough, er... Not enough..." she struggled for the word as she pointed angrily at her feet. "Not enough *Go Button*!"

"Exactly," I smiled with her at her creativity "Doesn't matter what you call it so long as *you* know what you mean."

Being put in sudden, quick-fire answer situations seemed to shake her vocabulary slightly although her message and underlying meaning was always crystal clear.

During a lesson to consolidate her use of mirrors, one of her few weak driving points, I asked her, as we were approaching a narrow situation between parked cars on either side of the road and toward oncoming traffic (i.e. a hazardous situation!) what her first reaction should be.

Knowing the answer because she executed the situation perfectly but stumbling over the words, her amusing and immediate retort was simply, "Oh my God!"

These light-hearted moments kept the lessons fun and Julia even seemed pleased with her instant embellishments to the English language.

Flushed with my test success over the preceding weeks and Julia's rapid progress, I soon found myself at the test centre again and calmly standing before the poster-plastered notice board as Julia confidently took a seat and began texting with her thumbs at the speed of a high court stenographer.

Julia had insisted upon an early morning test at the beginning of the month as she had heard – as have many other pupils it seems – that if you get an early test, early in the week and at the beginning of a month, then the quota of passes that the examiners have been given have not been reached and so she has a better chance to pass.

The myth that, once the quota has been reached, no matter how good you drive, you will not pass, is a difficult one to shake. It *is* just a myth created by disgruntled candidates to excuse their failure but seems now to have become an urban "truth" as 90% of my pupils will ask me about it sometime during their lessons.

Obviously my honest face isn't convincing enough when I assure them it is not true, or maybe they are just leaving the door ajar just in case they fail too. Whichever is the case, the myth perpetuates in spite of the official

DSA denial printed on the back of the test invitation letter.

Hence, I find myself in the test centre at 07.50h on the 1st June. A bright, cold but sunny summer's morning!

The whole atmosphere had changed in the test centre which, although still distinctly shabby, now took on a brighter, less soviet feel with the sunlight.

"Don't forget to vote for your ADI of the year!" my eye caught the slightly sunlight-faded headline, so I read on as I briefly considered myself as an outside contender before regaining my senses. "Get your vote in by October 31st and your choice could be crowned UK ADI of the year 2004, by Christmas."

"2004!" I blurted out loud but no one else in the room flickered from their nervous shoe-staring and Julia continued her rapid, Morse code-like clicks on her Blackberry.

Below the long outdated poster hung many more singularly pinned A4 sheets. Some printed, some handwritten but all in various states of curling in on their central fastenings.

As a rule of thumb it seemed that the more they were curled, the older they were and, as I inserted my fingers between the tightest paper tubes and spread them open, I caught sight of the tell-tale glimpses of long since past dates of notices and requests ranging from:

"Please avoid excessive use of Alton Mews for manoeuvres" to

"You must submit your paperwork before Easter for your mandatory CRB check" and even a handwritten note from the Chief Examiner asking, "Please refrain from using propane language in this waiting room!" by which I guess they were referring to incendiary comments uttered by candidates following a test failure.

A broad smile crossed my face at my razor-sharp wit and turning to Julia to share my humorous discovery I bumped my forehead on the stiff leather rough cloth rim of a Lowry-style cap and immediately recognised the blood-red checked shirt of Victor Faylum. Not six inches from my face, and only held at this distance by his flat brown brim, he stood rigidly with his grey eyes burning unamused contempt into mine.

"Julia Jimenez," he whispered, spitting an especially hard J for both names without moving his fixed gaze from me.

Immediately the click-clack of Julia's snake dancing thumbs froze in the otherwise silent room and my smiling face physically dropped several millimetres into a closed mouth gulp.

During the intervening months I had almost forgotten about Mr Faylum. Although always a nagging possibility in every instructor's mind when we brought a candidate for a "practical", I had not even seen him since the baptism of fire of my first two tests and suppose I had become lax. The reality was now all the more horrific for that complacency!

The petit, dark Julia looked pensively up from her well-worked phone and I could immediately see that she caught my sinking feeling.

Mr F swung away from me and, in an instant, adopted a politician-style "genuine" smile that seemed more to do with his anticipation at receiving another victim than with friendliness and Julia nervously rose to introduce herself with a gently lisped accented, "Good morning Sir."

Needless to say, Faylum ignored her greeting and waffled blindly through his required speech.

By this time the rules had changed slightly and, although he tried to sidestep the option, Julia overheard the other examiners, who by now had filled the waiting room, ask if the other pupils would like to bring their instructors with them as observers, and asked, "Can I bring my instructor too please?"

Faylum's false grin fell to his default scowl and he slowly threw a head to foot sneer of distain over me. "Whatever you like," were his only words as he turned away from us both.

Once in the car, Faylum turned to me and delivered to me his usual, "Not a peep!" warning but with an unexpected additional order. "and sit behind me, not Julia," he demanded.

"Why?" I questioned and began to explain but was interrupted with, "One, because I said so and two, because you can clearly see the mistakes Julia makes."

"But…" I tried and failed again and was taken aback by his assumption that Julia was going to make mistakes. Hardly a fair and open-minded approach, I thought, and feared that it leant toward a pre-determined result.

"I told you why. Do it or the test stops here," he threatened, before mumbling, what I suspect was, his real motive, "and I don't want you looking over my shoulder."

I did as I was told.

Julia, a confident driver, normally anyway, did well. She seemed to be able to ignore his provocative rudeness and I was pleased that she held her concentration well and, as the end of the test approached, I felt sure that even Faylum could not find fault in her driving.

I was right. She passed!

But I was both amazed and dismayed at how he still turned what should have been a moment of joy to remember for the rest of her life, into a negative lecture.

"I'm afraid to say you've passed," were his dejected words and for a second his negative tone threw both of us.

Then we realised the truth and Julia let out a yelp of glee.

"Okay, that's enough nonsense," he raised his voice. "This doesn't mean that you're a good driver."

Julia's face blushed with instant anger and her Latin temperament hardened her eyes.

"In fact I don't feel safe in the car with you."

"And I don't feel safe with you either, creepy man!" her soft accent snarled back and I thought, good on you girl.

We were both dumbstruck again however, by Mr F's retort. "Try not to be rude. It's not clever and the DSA will not tolerate verbal abuse of its staff. You must have seen the posters in the waiting room."

Hypocrisy over, he returned to his begrudging and clearly disappointed, "I have to pass you because I did not see any mistakes but to be honest, you know that you are not very good."

I could feel Julia's rage building like an overheating engine in the, already nerve-warmed car, but apparently oblivious he continued with his antagonism and upped the stakes by including me too.

"For example, when you made your reverse park, you stopped at one point to look over your shoulder. That is wrong."

Julia looked back at me as I shook my head and mouthed a big "no" but, still scared to speak until the certificate was signed and in Julia's hands, I said nothing audible.

Determined to prompt a response though, our examiner continued without looking up from the frantic ticking and signing of his paperwork, "so if your instructor told you that, then you ought to have changed him long ago."

The car was silent for what seemed like hours whilst Julia waited for Faylum to complete the Pass Certificate and, in some way, his last, over the top, black-cloaked villain comments helped both of us see the funny side. Now we were both in this together and he had become a cartoon baddy.

The other main redeeming feature of the situation that we both picked up on was that Victor Faylum, despite his best efforts, had failed to provoke either of us thereby magnifying his disappointment at having to pass someone.

"And," Julia added, "I told you that I would pass if I took my test early in the month!"

Although my reputation was slowly and steadily building, already a move that initially seemed like I had arrived in ADI heaven now, and only one month after the mugging I had suffered at the hands of The PAs, appeared to confirm my worst fears

Having received exactly 30 leads in my first two weeks, from which I had managed to glean just 11, I received only 7 more throughout the rest of the year.

My latest bid for the outside lane found me still trying to get off the hard shoulder and seemed to be just one shift of gear up to the inevitable driving instructor's goal.

Working independently.

Printed in Great Britain
by Amazon.co.uk, Ltd.,
Marston Gate.